Praise for the book

In today's fast-changing world, effective communication has become very important to bring about international understanding. Through *Listening for Well-Being*, Arun has drawn upon his experiences and encounters to highlight the lost art of listening. Each chapter uncovers a different facet associated with listening, pushing back stereotypes to bring about change through dialogue. His insights, peppered with anecdotes, provide a unique perspective on collaborative solutions aimed at addressing humanity's greatest challenges.

Ratan Tata, *Chairman emeritus, Tata Sons*

There is a lot that is serious, entertaining, profound and useful in this highly readable book. It ranges over the big, profound questions of the fate of the liberal order or of democracy, while not missing out on the very important minutiae of how tables and chairs need to be arranged to guarantee a dialogue where people not only talk to each other, but listen to each other as well. Read this book and learn how many of our daily problems come from talking but not listening.

Lord Meghnad Desai, *British parliamentarian and Chairman, Meghnad Desai Academy of Economics, Mumbai*

To look without seeing, hear without listening, and touch without feeling is what we do all the time. Arun Maira tells us what, as a result, we miss out on. To read this book is to open windows where only walls were, doors where only corners stood—dank, cob-webbed and cold. It enables us to hear the voices of our times, our peers and our alternatives through the din of our conditionings and the silence of our prejudices.

Prof. Gopalkrishna Gandhi, *Former administrator and diplomat, and former Governor of West Bengal*

Arun Maira has a great style of making serious points in a casual storytelling way. He tells us why listening to others is so vital. He explains how we can improve the quality of listening to improve the world and our own lives. We *must* listen to him.

Nobel laureate Muhammad Yunus, *Founder, Grameen Bank*

Also by the same author

Redesigning the Aeroplane While Flying: Reforming Institutions
An Upstart in Government: Journeys of Change and Learning

LISTENING
FOR WELL-BEING

LISTENING
FOR WELL-BEING

Conversations
with
People Not Like Us

ARUN MAIRA

Published by
Rupa Publications India Pvt. Ltd 2017
7/16, Ansari Road, Daryaganj
New Delhi 110002

Sales Centres:
Allahabad Bengaluru Chennai
Hyderabad Jaipur Kathmandu
Kolkata Mumbai

Copyright © Arun Maira 2017

Illustrations by Ritabrata Joardar

The views and opinions expressed in this book are the author's own and the facts are as reported by her which have been verified to the extent possible, and the publishers are not in any way liable for the same.

All rights reserved.
No part of this publication may be reproduced, transmitted, or stored in a retrieval system, in any form or by any means, electronic, mechanical, photocopying, recording or otherwise, without the prior permission of the publisher.

ISBN: 978-81-291-4821-6

First impression 2017

10 9 8 7 6 5 4 3 2 1

The moral right of the author has been asserted.

Printed and bound in India by Replika Press Pvt. Ltd.

This book is sold subject to the condition that it shall not, by way of trade or otherwise, be lent, resold, hired out, or otherwise circulated, without the publisher's prior consent, in any form of binding or cover other than that in which it is published.

To my grandchildren
Viren, Aarti and Layla

Listening

It is time to press the pause button; put our smartphones on silent;
Shut out the tweets, trolls and soundbites;
And stop the windmills in our minds.
It is time to listen.
To listen to the whispers in the trees; the caring in our hearts;
And most of all, to the voices of people not like us.
Then, we will learn and find solutions for living together on our shared Earth.

CONTENTS

Foreword		*xiii*
The Power of Listening		*xv*
1.	We the People	1
2.	We are Not Listening	21
3.	Listening to People Not Like Us	33
4.	Why is it So Difficult to Listen to People Not Like Us?	49
5.	Spaces for Good Conversations	57
6.	Lenses and Stereotypes	67
7.	Building and Crossing Bridges	97
8.	The Pillars of the Bridge: Richness in Conversations	107
9.	The Spans of the Bridge: Part A—The Media	123
10.	The Spans of the Bridge: Part B—Democratic Deliberations	141
11.	Shaping Our Future Together	159
Epilogue: Am I Listening?		163
Acknowledgements		171
Index		175

FOREWORD

I am happy that Mr Arun Maira, a distinguished academician, has written this concise book entitled *Listening for Well-Being*. As the title says, the book provides insight into the relationship between listening and well-being of individuals.

Indeed, listening is the first of the three wisdom tools in Buddhist tradition, the other two being contemplating and meditating; it is the gateway to improving oneself, both mentally and physically. Listening, without preconceived notion and with respect and full attention, is the way to understand each other. This is the real way to communicate on issues without any distortion.

Through proper listening, followed by proper analysis and practice, one can develop positive attributes like love and compassion. This can lead to inner tranquillity and a peaceful mind. All of these will have an impact on the well-being of individuals as well as society at large. The more we care for the happiness of others, the greater will be our own feeling of well-being.

As long as we live in this world we are bound to encounter problems. If, at such times, we lose hope and become discouraged, we diminish our ability to face difficulties. If, on the other hand, we adopt the right attitude and have a more realistic perspective, it will increase our determination and capacity to overcome challenges. Indeed, with this attitude, each new obstacle can be seen as yet another valuable opportunity to improve our mind!

His Holiness the Dalai Lama
25 May 2017

THE POWER OF LISTENING

To know how to love someone, we have to understand them. To understand, we need to listen.

—Thich Nhat Hanh

I became acutely aware of the transformative power of deep listening 40 years ago. I learned about this power from a Jesuit priest who helped me with a very difficult conflict. I was the youngest member of a team of managers building India's first indigenous truck factory. I was responsible for the 'human side of the enterprise'—for finding the people we needed; to develop a spirit of continuous learning; and to facilitate a culture of teamwork. My colleagues on the management team, all older and more experienced than me, were responsible for the actual work of planning, building and running the factory.

The engineers and managers at Tata Motors (then known as Tata Engineering and Locomotive Company—Telco in short) were under great pressure in the 1970s to learn to do things they had never done before. The company went into the business of manufacturing trucks and buses in India in 1954. It acquired the know-how from Daimler Benz of Germany. When the technical collaboration with Daimler Benz expired in 1969,

THE POWER OF LISTENING

Telco had to develop its technology and expand its business on its own. For this, it decided to put up new facilities in Pune, near Mumbai. These facilities included an R&D centre along with new factories for manufacturing trucks. The project became very challenging because the Government of India, faced with a foreign exchange crunch, curbed the import of machines, press dies, and equipment that Telco needed. Since such machines and dies were not obtainable in India, the company had to manufacture them for itself. Telco's engineers and managers had to learn to do this while they were setting up and running an automobile factory, a challenging task in itself. As one of them said, 'It seemed they were designing and building an aircraft while they were flying it!'

There were many things to be learned and coordinated. To ensure that the Pune projects were completed in time and within budget, R&D engineers had to get the designs of the trucks right, machine and die designers had to get the machines and dies right, and the production staff, working with the outputs of these 'first-timers', had to produce truck parts to specified quality standards, within cost and on time—about which there could be no compromise. It did not help that the truck market went into recession as the Pune plant was coming up, putting pressure to reduce the costs of the project and of the trucks. All this created immense tension in the organization in Pune. When things went wrong (and in the difficult conditions in which people were working, many things seemed to go wrong), tempers flared up. When one day, the manager of the foundry and the general manager had a violent argument on the shop floor in front of their startled workers, I knew that I was beyond my depth and needed an expert's help to improve relationships within the management team.

Someone gave me the idea of inviting an American Jesuit priest, Father Joe Curry, who was in India at the time and had conducted some programmes on counselling for managers elsewhere. Joe Curry had been trained in Chicago in the techniques of 'non-directive counselling' developed by Carl Rogers. He agreed to run a two-day workshop for Telco's senior managers.

The manager who was under the most stress at that time was the chief of the new foundry being established in Pune. His foundry was built with equipment that had been designed within Telco, by people with no prior experience in doing so. Moreover, his young team of engineers and workmen operating that equipment had hardly any experience of working in a foundry. When the truck production lines stopped, it was very often a problem with the castings made in the foundry and it was he who had to face the music. Though he was most reluctant to be away from the foundry for two days, he was persuaded to attend the programme to ensure that the entire management team could be together.

Something remarkable happened in the programme. Joe Curry began by introducing some concepts, and then played an audio tape of an amusing speech by a famous American psychotherapist, Dr Murray Banks. By this time, the foundry manager was beginning to get very fidgety. This seemed to be a total waste of his time. He let Joe Curry know this. He asked

THE POWER OF LISTENING

how concepts that Joe brought from the United States (US) could be relevant to the very different and tough conditions in India. As he vented out his frustration, everyone else was embarrassed because Joe had made a great effort to come for the programme. But everybody was silent, even though many others, by now, also felt that Joe may not have anything useful for them.

Joe listened very calmly and extremely attentively to the foundry manager. With a gentle nod and with sympathy in his eyes, Joe acknowledged the manager's pain and anger, and walked towards him. The manager continued venting. Both looked each other in the eye—one with anger; the other with empathy. Joe did not defend the utility of the ideas he had brought, but simply acknowledged the manager's emotions. Some minutes later, the manager stopped his tirade. By now, both seemed oblivious to the others in the room. There was silence for several seconds, though it seemed like several minutes. The manager became very still. He said very quietly to Joe, 'I think you know how I feel.' Joe nodded slightly and continued to look the manager in the eye, but gently. He did not say a word. A few seconds later, the manager said, 'This is the first time in a long while that I have felt that someone has *really* listened to me. Thank you.'

Joe returned to his presentation. But the manager was not paying attention to Joe's words any more. He continued to look towards Joe, as if in a reverie. The rest of us were also unable to hear Joe: we had been so taken up by what we had seen. Joe smiled and asked, 'What is going on in your minds?' With that, we went into our first lesson—the power of listening deeply. Joe taught us to pay attention to the feelings of the person speaking and to acknowledge them. He taught us to focus on the other person, rather than on ourselves—our own anger and hurt or joy—and not on the points we would make to counter the attack on us.

As the lesson progressed, the foundry manager said to Joe, 'I must have hurt you. You came here to help as best you could. Yet, I vented my frustration onto you. What were your feelings?' Joe maintained that his instant reaction had been that he was being targeted unfairly. But then, he said he began to concentrate on the manager's anger and wondered why he was so angry. He became curious about the manager's story. That was the look of empathetic enquiry that all of us, including the manager, had noticed in Joe's eyes. Joe asked the manager, 'Do you recall what you were thinking when you stopped speaking and became silent?' The manager said, 'Yes, I was thinking that you might be genuinely interested in my story, and that perhaps, I would like to share it with you. It is a feeling I have not had with anyone for months.'

I was so struck. I had spent many hours with the foundry manager, counselling him in my own way, which was to speak to him and give him advice and reassurance. Yet, a total stranger, without uttering a word, had made a connection at a public meeting in just a few minutes, something that I had been unable to establish after hours of effort in one-to-one conversations. An American, who was not familiar to us, brought us so much to learn from! Here it was—the power of listening.

THE POWER OF LISTENING

The day after the workshop, I gratefully invited Joe to my house for lunch with my wife. She and our cook, Augustin, had prepared a very nice meal. When Augustin came to serve us, Joe thanked him and asked him his name. In the next three minutes, a conversation took place between Joe and Augustin as if there was no one else in the room. Joe looked Augustin directly in his eyes and listened intently. Augustin spoke and revealed a side of himself that I had never known, even though Augustin had worked with us for more than five years!

In the two days he was with us, Joe gave me some tips to improve my listening with the principles of Carl Rogers' 'non-directive counselling'. The only objective the listener must have is to understand the other person. There should be no desire to direct the conversation to achieve any other objective; no desire to convince the other person of one's own point of view; no desire to prove the other person wrong and no desire to win any argument. The only objective must be to listen to the other person's feelings and to understand his point of view. In yoga, one is taught to breathe out completely in order to create a vacuum in one's body, which is filled in by a refreshing new breath. Similarly, in deep listening, one must practice the 'breathing out' of any desire to direct the conversation, so that one can 'breathe in' the point of view of the other. Yoga helps to refresh one's own body and mind, whereas in non-directive listening, one can refresh another person's mind, just like Joe did during his interaction with the foundry manager. There is therapeutic value in the stillness of one's own mind also when one is deeply listening to another.

LISTENING FOR WELL-BEING

Joe's lessons on how to listen to another helped me greatly in my professional work. I was expected to counsel senior managers when they had performance issues. Rather than telling them what was wrong with them, I found the meetings became much more productive when I gently prodded the managers with questions about how they were feeling, and then let them talk. They were far more likely to take responsibility for their own actions than if I tried to convince them with facts and arguments, as I was wont to until Joe's workshop.

I was expected to light a fire in the belly of the young Indians we were hiring to enable Telco realize its ambition to build the first completely indigenous truck factory. Rather than lecture them about their responsibility for India's future, I found it much more effective to ask them what they aspired to achieve the most in their lives. And then listen to them—and let them listen to their own aspirations too.

I was responsible for relations between the union and the management, and strengthening the cooperation between workmen and managers, so that together we could do what had not been done in India so far, viz. setup an Indian truck factory built entirely by Indians. New work practices and mindsets were necessary. And work was hard. There were many conflicts and many occasions for tough negotiations between the union and the management. On one such occasion, the president of the workmen's union came to give me an ultimatum. His body language was belligerent. I asked him to sit down, and I let him talk, like Joe Curry had let the foundry manager talk. I showed no desire to make him change his mind. After many minutes, he stopped. He said this was not the sort of conversation he had expected to have. I paraphrased what I had heard him say so far, without any evaluative comments. He then said to me what the foundry manager had said to Joe. That it was the first time that a senior manager had *really* listened to him. He said, 'You are different. Maybe we can work well together.'

Twenty years later, in the 1990s, I began consulting with automobile companies in the US to improve their competiveness vis-à-vis Japanese companies, who were expanding in the US market. My clients were the largest automobile assemblers and automobile parts producers in the world. They believed that an Indian manager, who had so far worked all his life in India, could teach them precious little about the technical and financial aspects of their operations. But I found that there was something unique I was able to offer. It was the ability to listen to everyone in their enterprises. I would begin my consulting engagements with a diagnosis of the human side of the enterprise. I listened to workers in night shifts in plants in Detroit and Philadelphia that were facing threats of closure. Usually, these were older workers, and many blacks too, who the management regarded as an obstacle in improving the productivity. Initially, the workers would wonder who I was and what I was up to—a middle-aged Indian man willing to sit around in a night shift. Some others would come by and make enquiries about my identity. In turn, I would ask them about their histories and their hopes for their future. From those conversations came ideas for better partnerships between workmen and managers.

LISTENING FOR WELL-BEING

One thing often leads to another. Soon, I was consulting for leaders of several organizations in the US, Europe and Latin America, on ways to tone up their enterprises into 'learning organizations' in which all members, bottom to top, worked together to improve the performance of the company. To think and work together, they had to learn to listen to each other. Along the way, I learned the art of systems thinking and deeper listening from many masters of these arts—Peter Senge, Bryan Smith, Charlie Kiefer, Jenny Kemeny, Peter Stroh, and others. They were guiding lights of Innovation Associates (which I briefly managed) and the International Society of Organizational Learning.

On my return to India, my endeavours to learn to listen, and to listen to learn, continued into larger and more complex enterprises. I facilitated three rounds of scenario building exercises for India, in which hundreds of very diverse people from different walks of life participated. They listened to each other and saw many facets of their remarkably diverse country. They collectively envisioned desirable paths to its future through the mists of inevitable uncertainties. I also worked for five years as a Member of India's Planning Commission, where I experienced, first hand, the need for and the difficulties in creating collaboration amongst many stakeholders for the country's progress. Ever since I became aware of the intricacies of deep listening forty years ago, I have often observed how shallowly people listen to each other. In fact, I sometimes even catch myself not really listening! I have noticed that when people don't listen to each other, they cannot come to agreements. At most, they may agree to disagree. Since they do not listen well, they cannot understand each other's perspectives and find mutually acceptable solutions. One side may force a solution on the other, if it has the power to do so. But the conflict remains. It merely goes underground, and then resurfaces in other forms.

By listening to others, we improve their feeling of well-being, as Joe Curry did for Telco's foundry manager. I have learned that when I listen deeply to others, I also improve my own feeling of well-being.

Listening is a simple idea. Everyone—rich or poor, powerful or weak, educated or uneducated—can listen to others, regardless of whether they are rich or poor, powerful or weak, educated or uneducated. Listening seems like a very small thing. Yet, I believe it has enormous power to change the world.

The inability of people to listen to each other has immense consequences for humanity. *Can We Save True Dialogue in an Age of Mistrust?* published by Dag Hammarskjold Foundation, is a record of conversations sixty years ago between two remarkable persons: Dag Hammarskjold, the second Secretary General of the UN, and Martin Buber, the great Jewish philosopher. It notes:

> The Cold War has ended, but the atmosphere of mistrust prevails. The crucial question of the Middle East remains unresolved. Only the concept of what constitutes the enemy has changed: fundamental terrorism has replaced the Soviet Union as a challenge for the West, while the

West's answer to all challenges remains war—the opposite of the word.[1]

These two remarkable men commented on the condition of strife in the world six decades ago. The strife continues. There was euphoria when the Soviet Union collapsed in 1991. Perhaps there would be no more monumental strife, because the ideologies of liberal democracy and free markets (that the US-led West propagated) had won. It was the 'end of history', as American political scientist Francis Fukuyama had famously declared. Since then, the Internet has expanded around the world and six years ago, social media seemed to give another big boost to the overthrow of authoritarian regimes and the spread of democracy during the Arab Spring.

It is remarkable how quickly history has returned after it was supposed to have ended a mere quarter of a century ago. In his 2008 book *The Return of History and the End of Dreams*, American historian Robert Kagan maintained that geopolitics was back on stage and great powers were once again competing for honour and influence.[2]

The Internet and social media were assumed to be benign forces that would bring the world together. Like all powerful technologies, they can do great good, as well as great harm. Now

---

[1] *Can We Save True Dialogue in an Age of Mistrust: The Encounters of Dag Hammarskjold and Martin Buber; Critical Currents*, Dag Hammarskjold Foundation, Occasional Paper Series no. 8, January 2010.
[2] Kagan, Robert, *The Return of History and the End of Dreams*, Alfred A. Knopf, 2008.

the dark side of the Internet and social media has emerged. They are being used by terrorists to execute their campaigns. Governments are using them for surveillance of citizens. Another realization is that social media has a detrimental impact on the quality of interpersonal relationships. It has also contributed to an increasing shallowness, as well as viciousness in public discourse, and has divided people, whereas it was widely believed that it would bring people together into one global united world.

Equally disturbing is the emerging evidence of the disillusionment of young people with democracy in the US and other countries that were supposed to be the champions for spreading and protecting democracy around the world. While the US and the European Union (EU) continue to propagate democratic values worldwide, citizens within these countries, especially young people, are losing faith in democracy. Roberto Foa and Yascha Mounk in 'The Democratic Disconnect', *Journal of Democracy*, have analysed the results of World Values Surveys over many years. To the question, 'Is it essential to live in a country that is governed democratically?' only 30 per cent of US citizens born after 1980 said 'yes' (compared to 50 per cent of those born in the 1950s and 75 per cent born in the 1930s). In Europe, 45 per cent—less than half—of those born after 1980 replied in the affirmative, compared to 55 per cent of those born in the 1960s. The disenchantment of citizens of all ages with democratic government has increased since 1995 in the US. In 1995, 17 per cent of 16 to 24-year-olds said that 'Having a democratic political system is a "bad" or "very bad" way to run a country,' 24 per cent felt that way in 2011. In 1995, only 5 per cent of citizens over 65 years in the US were disenchanted with democracy. By 2011, that number had increased to 12 per cent.[3]

While democracies are fraying, environmental degradation, depletion of fresh water resources and climate change continue. The Club of Rome, which was founded in 1968, described itself as 'a group of world citizens, sharing a common concern for the future of humanity'. Fifty years ago, it warned that the prevalent materialistic paradigm of progress would soon hit 'limits to growth', with the inability of the Earth to renew itself and to continue supporting the increasing pressure humanity was putting on it. Its warnings have been dismissed as false alarms. Even now, some business and political leaders, in the US and elsewhere too, insist that climate change is a hoax. Fortunately, there is growing realization around the world at last that we cannot carry on the way we are.

But what has listening got to do with all this, you may ask? Quite a lot, as I will explain in this book.

All countries have agreed to cooperate to achieve 17 Sustainable Development Goals. These goals cover, fairly comprehensively, global concerns of environmental sustainability, persistent poverty and inequity. Achievement of these goals will require cooperation amongst people with many different perspectives—environmentalists, industrialists, humanists, scientists, and others. They will require cooperation

---

[3] "The Democratic Disconnect", *Journal of Democracy*, Vol. 27, No. 3, July 2016.

amongst businesses, civil societies, governments and, above all, cooperation amongst nations. The eight Millennium Development Goals adopted by the United Nations in 2000 had similarly ambitious targets, which were expected to be achieved by 2015. They were not, and a review of the reasons revealed that the approach to global challenges must change. Solutions to global problems lie in local actions. They should not be, and cannot be, imposed top-down. Diverse stakeholders, who are often in contention, will have to collaborate with each other on the ground, and think and work together. They will have to listen to each other much better than they are doing now.

The profound question before humanity in the new millennium is, 'How on Earth can we live together harmoniously, and in harmony with the one Earth that we share?' An answer to the question is: by listening to each other deeply, understanding each other's perspectives, and finding inclusive and sustainable solutions for global challenges.

'Who are you writing this book for?' my publisher, Kapish Mehra, asked me. I am writing it for people everywhere who care about their families, their communities, and the condition of their environments. Because by listening to others better, and by helping to improve the quality of listening in conversations happening around them, they will improve the well-being of their families, their communities, their countries and the world.

'What sort of a book is it going to be?' he asked, 'A how-to-do-it, self-help book? Or a conceptual, academic book?' 'Both,' I said, 'I would like my readers to reflect with me about the state of the world and why we must improve the quality of conversation amongst people. I would also like to offer my readers some means for them to make a difference in the world.'

'Then you must include many stories in your book,' Kapish suggested. Stories make abstract ideas concrete. I do have many stories to tell—stories of conversations, or break-downs of conversations, in India and elsewhere. The preponderance of Indian stories in a book about diversity of people, differences in perspectives, and the urgent need to improve processes for democratic deliberation, cannot be a bad thing. India is the most diverse country in the world, in terms of languages, religions and races of its citizens. The Indian Constitution demands that its citizens treat each other as equals and govern themselves democratically. It is a wonderful laboratory for democratic dialogue amongst diverse people.

The first chapter analyses some major global issues. There are many causes and many explanations for these complex issues. A principal difficulty in addressing them is the increasing tension between nation states, which are tightening the boundaries around themselves. People are retreating into their own identities, are becoming less willing to accommodate others' needs and understand other perspectives. Within countries too, including my own India, the definition of who 'we Indians are' is becoming more exclusionary.

Chapters 2 to 7 explain why we find it so hard to listen to people who are not like us, and, therefore, what we need to change. We have different cultures, different histories and different types of education. They give us different 'lenses' through which we see the world, and see each other. Our lenses help us to focus on what we believe is important and what we consider right. But they limit our vision. We cannot rewrite our histories or shed our cultures suddenly. Therefore, we cannot change our deeply embedded lenses. Nor can we, or should we, change others' histories, cultures and lenses. We must respect each other. Together, by combining our different perspectives, we can see reality more completely.

The remaining chapters from 8 to 11 explain what we can and must change to improve our ability to listen to and understand people who are not like us. We can change the structures of our conversations and create spaces in which we are able to listen to each other better, less distracted by the stereotypes in our minds. We must also improve the quality of public discourse in the media (including social media).

I explain in these chapters that democracy cannot be limited only to the conduct of free and fair elections. Deep democracy also requires processes for dialogue amongst citizens. So long as we have nation states—and they are likely to be around for a long time—governments of the people will be electable only within the boundaries of nations. An election of a government of the whole world may be far in the future. Until then, democratic deliberation across national boundaries, between people who believe they are sovereign and have a right to follow their own traditions and to be who they are, must provide the glue to hold the world together.

This book is about ways to evoke and use the power of listening. It shows that by listening deeply, especially to people who are not like us, we can improve the world for everyone.

We must listen to people from other cultures and countries. We must listen to citizens within our own countries who have different views. We must listen to our neighbours. We must listen deeply to ourselves too.

The epilogue to the book has tips on how to listen deeply to others and ourselves.

1

WE THE PEOPLE

I am willing to serve my country; but my worship I reserve for Right which is far greater than my country. To worship my country as a god is to bring a curse upon it.

—Rabindranath Tagore, *The Home and the World*

When Brexit happened in June 2016, I was nestled safely in the Himalayas, where I had retreated from the scorching heat of Delhi. From news centres in London, Delhi and other places, the TV brought to me the bewilderment at the self-goal the British seemed to have scored. Business analysts were alarmed, and as confused as the downward squiggles of stock market indices on their TV screens in the aftermath of the exit.

DIFFERENT STORIES, DIFFERENT HISTORIES

My apartment is in Mashobra, Himachal Pradesh, on the side of a mountain on top of which the British had built a summer

WHO IS AN INDIAN?

retreat for their viceroys of India. The President of India uses the Retreat now. Below the President's Retreat, a large home is being built for Priyanka Gandhi, whose mother, father, grandmother and great-grandfather led the Congress Party for over 65 years after the British rulers left India. The President of India, and Priyanka Gandhi and her mother, Sonia Gandhi, visited Mashobra in June 2016, while I was there. I did not meet them. Though I met many 'aam aadmi' (common people) and listened to stories of their lives.

One was a woman cowherd, whom I encountered along with her husband. I saw them every morning along with their cow and a small calf when I walked along the road through the forest. While the animals grazed, they would gather leaves and grass in sacks. We greeted each other every day. She said they earned about ₹10,000 a month by selling milk. 'Not much, but enough, and life is not bad,' she said.

Another was Mandeep, the young carpenter whose services we needed to pull down our ceiling and clean out the mess that pigeons had made in our rafters. Mandeep had been an assistant to the old village carpenter, and was now trying to establish his own carpentry business. With the booming construction of summer homes on the steep Mashobra hillside, a carpenter is in great demand. Mandeep's cell phone was ringing all the time, with irate customers demanding that he show up immediately. He could not be at so many places at the same time; so he would patiently apologize and promise to come very soon. Mandeep's aspiration was to go to the US where, he heard, tradesmen like him were treated with respect and lived in big homes alongside their customers' homes.

I helped Mandeep's assistant, an older man, to finish the work in our apartment as quickly as possible. The assistant carried Mandeep's tools, held the ladder while he worked, and cleaned up after the work was done. The assistant was completely unskilled. He had never used a screwdriver or spanner, and did not know the very basics—that these tools are always turned clockwise to tighten screws and bolts. Mandeep had put him to work to scrape off traces of varnish on the window glasses with a razor blade. I picked up a blade and began scraping along with him. He paused, and watched me—an old, balding, grey-haired man—handling the blade very well. He said, with admiration, 'You must have been very clever when you were young!'

Sitting on my balcony, beneath the Retreat of viceroys and presidents, turning away from the breaking news and soundbites on TV, and looking out over the valley to the ranges of Himalayas rising higher and higher into the distance, I reflected on the longue durée (long waves) of history. Long waves in India's political history: its colonial past, its long dominance by Indira Gandhi's family, and now into another era. Long waves in European history: the Peace of Westphalia, the scientific Enlightenment, two horrible world wars, followed by the rise of the EU, and now Brexit.

Life has been very good to me. I had opportunities to learn, work, and fulfil my aspirations that my fellow Indians—Mandeep and his assistant, and the cowherd and her husband—never had. It was amply clear from my conversations with them, and with many other aam aadmis on forest paths and in Mashobra that despite living in the same place, mentally we inhabit very different worlds. The actors and events in the big stories in their heads about their world did not include Donald Trump, Brexit, or oscillations of global stock indices, which were the subjects of almost all conversations amongst the 'people like us', who had come to Mashobra to escape India's summer heat.

What is the history of India? What is the history of the world? From whose perspectives should we record history? Theirs or Ours? What should history be about? Should it be about the rise and decline of dynasties, and the lives of important people who occupy high places, or the changes in the patterns of livelihoods of common people like the cowherd and her husband, and Mandeep and his assistant? Should history record the changes in the GDPs of countries and rise of Asian economies, or the rise and decline of forests, the evidence of which I could see on the mountain ranges before me? And what about the history of the rise and decline of ideas that drive our institutions and our collective actions—such as beliefs in communism and capitalism, and globalization and the nation state?

Amongst the books I had taken to read in Mashobra was Immanuel Wallerstein's *World-Systems Analysis*. Wallerstein writes:

> It is important to look anew not only at how the world in which we live works but also how we have come to think about this world...The emergence of this mode of

analysis is a reflection of, and expression of, the real protest about the deep inequalities of the world-system that are so politically central to our current times.

Are we listening when people speak? It is high time we listen to people not like us and examine the 'theories-in-use' in our heads about governance of societies and economies. I will mention three here.

The first is the idea of growth. Amongst 'people like us', 'growth' has become shorthand for growth of GDP only. Whereas human beings value growth in many other things that matter to them, which philosopher Michael Sandel explains in his book *What Money Can't Buy: The Moral Limits of Markets*.[1] These include our dignity, fairness in society, security in our lives, sustainability of environmental resources, and happiness. However, these qualities that we value so much in our lives and societies are not measurable in monetary terms. Therefore, they are excluded from conventional economic measures of growth. In fact, many activities that contribute to the growth of GDP seem to destroy things that we would like to have more of, such as more sustainability of the environment and more harmony in society.

The second is the idea of how a global world should be governed. In one view, a complex system, such as the world, must be controlled centrally or there will be chaos. In this view, everyone must follow the same rules. The complication

---

[1] Sandel, Michael J., *What Money Can't Buy: The Moral Limits of Markets*, Farrar, Straus and Giroux, 2012.

lies in who makes the rules and how they are made. Those presently in power, in their rational self-interest, will argue for rules that will protect their sources of power, while others may feel their interests are not being sufficiently considered. This is the fundamental problem in the governance of most global institutions, such as the WTO, the UN's Security Council and the NSG (Nuclear Suppliers Group). This has also been the problem in the EU that has made many of its members unhappy, and which led to Brexit.

An analysis of these governance issues and suggestions for their resolution are given by Dani Rodrik in *The Globalization Paradox: Democracy and the Future of the World Economy*[2] and by Immanuel Wallerstein, Randall Collins, Michael Mann, Georgi Derluguian and Craig Calhoun in *Does Capitalism have a Future?*[3] The analysis suggests that while we are all part of one world, we must give freedom to people to design policies that fit their local realities to produce the best outcome for everyone.

The third is the concept of good governance. Governance is the process by which a society establishes the rules of the game and finds just solutions to its complex and contentious problems. In one view, a society is governed well when it is orderly, with everything under control, and with experts. In another view, good governance requires that processes for establishing the

---

[2] Rodrik, Dani, *The Globalization Paradox: Democracy and the Future of the World Economy*, W.W. Norton & Co., 2011.
[3] Wallerstein, Immanuel; Collins Randall; Mann, Michael; Derluguian, Georgi M.; Calhoun, Craig, *Does Capitalism Have a Future?*, Oxford University Press, 2014.

rules of the game must be transparent, participative and effective. This is a vision of a deliberative democracy, in which citizens are informed and made to understand the implications of the decisions they are being asked to take and support. Merely letting people make big decisions (like Brexit) by voting may seem very democratic. But it is not good governance 'of the people by the people', if people do not understand what is at stake. Therefore, innovations are required in processes of democratic deliberation to enable informed participation of citizens. Indeed, this is the twenty-first century challenge in the evolution of better systems of governance.

Any technology can be used for good or for evil. Dynamite, nuclear energy and gene technology are some examples that have increased the ability of humans to change the world. Whether they have positive or negative affects depends upon how they are used and who uses them. Similarly, the Internet and social media can be enablers of good citizen participation. At the same time, these tools can stimulate more division and hate in society, as witnessed when they have been used by the ISIS and others.

Technology is not a panacea. Technology deployed in social media has given public conversations enormous reach. But it is also diminishing the richness of conversations, connecting and dividing us at the same time. Good processes must be designed and managed for citizen participation so that social media and the Internet enable good democratic deliberations.

GOVERNING OUR LIVES

Both the EU and India are ideas of diverse people coming closer to shape better futures together. The EU began as an economic union that has struggled with issues of political union. India was formed as a political union after its independence from Britain, and is now struggling to form its states into one common market with a uniform national tax on movement of goods and services throughout the union. Both Europe and India are trying to deepen their internal unions of nations and states. They have to strengthen systems for creating common rules; in the process, the parts must give up some of their independence to determine their own rules. Processes of centralization and homogenization, to create one from many, alienate people from their distant rulers who write the rules that people must live by. They also fear loss of their particular identities in a wider identity.

Processes of combining and centralizing, for obtaining larger economic benefits, run counter to the demands for self-determination and democracy. The latter is a rising longue durée in human history that shows no sign of ebbing. People in India would say *Dilli dur ast* (Delhi is still far away) when the Mughals ruled. 'Our rulers do not know us; we do not know them. They are far away.' When Mahatma Gandhi demanded rights to self-determination for Indians, Winston Churchill said that India, without (supposedly) good governance from London, would become a mess. Gandhi's retort was, 'At least, it will be our own mess.' Brussels is not as far from Britain as London is from India. Nevertheless, a majority of British citizens want freedom from their European rulers to make their own rules and to recover their own British identity. Strains to unravel unions, from people who want their right to self-determination, are going deeper within countries too. Within Britain, the Scots are straining at the bit. In India, Kashmiris continue their struggle.

Brexit revealed the disaffection of British citizens for the policies of their own government, which followed the fashions of globalization, free trade, corporate capitalism, and financialization of economies that have swept the world. Those policies have increased inequalities within societies, unemployment of young people, and have squeezed the middle class. The surprising popularity of Donald Trump and Bernie Sanders in the US has revealed the disaffection of both Republican and Democratic Party supporters for the ruling establishment of political and corporate leaders. Hillary Clinton was painted by Trump (and Sanders too) as a representative of *that* establishment. When she won her party's nomination and the support of Sanders, she felt compelled to indicate her opposition to ideologies of free trade, corporate capitalism and globalization. Trump defeated Clinton to become president of the US. Struggling to deliver his campaign promise to his supporters to clean up the 'Washington swamp'—as he described the political establishment—he appears so far to have been overwhelmed by it.

Citizens in electoral democracies are given the right to vote to choose their governments. But that is no longer enough, they say. They insist that they are being shut out of the processes by which major decisions that govern their lives are taken. Their government is 'of the people', but now they want a government 'by the people' too.

The Constitution of India, promulgated after India's independence from the British rule 70 years ago, granted universal franchise to all citizens, men and women, rich and poor, educated and illiterate. India's founding fathers believed that regardless of their circumstances, all human beings have equal rights to determine the way they shall be governed. In the Indian Constitution, the cowherd and her husband, Mandeep and his assistant, I, and other 'people like us', who travel the world and spend summers in Mashobra, are equals.

The same day, 8 November 2016, that Donald Trump was elected as the president of the US, Prime Minister Modi announced a sweeping 'demonetization' of the Indian economy. Five hundred rupee notes, which were widely used, would no longer be legal currency. Citizens were required to deposit their old notes in banks and collect new two-thousand-rupee notes, if they needed cash. However, the supply of new notes was very limited and so citizens were left without cash to pay for their daily groceries. Small enterprises were unable to pay their workers and their suppliers. Construction workers could not be paid their salaries and so construction activities came to a halt. Economists said Mr Modi had seriously wounded the Indian economy and the GDP would suffer as a result.

The immediate pain of demonetization was felt most acutely by people at the bottom of the economic pyramid, who did not have credit cards and needed cash to purchase their daily necessities. They stood in queues for hours outside banks to deposit whatever old notes they had, hoping to get some new notes which were very hard to come by. Elections to the state legislatures of several states were due in a couple of months, especially the large and economically not-so-well-off state of Uttar Pradesh. Most political analysts opined that Mr Modi had not only hurt the economy, but had made a huge political blunder. They said the very people whose votes he needed—the poorer sections of the population—were the most hurt by his so-called 'surgical strike' against black money and corruption. Some even expected the masses to revolt.

It did not happen. Poor people stood in lines patiently because they believed that demonetization would hurt the rich who had made a lot of money by corrupt means, often at the cost of poor people. Mr Modi called upon the poor people to undergo the hardships they were enduring as a sacrifice to create a more just and better world for themselves. He used the analogy of Mahatma Gandhi's mass non-violent movements to protest the oppression of colonial rulers. Many poor people suffered economically by Modi's surgical demonetization. However, they were made to believe that their sacrifice was for a larger cause of societal justice.

I listened to many 'people like us', cocooned in comfortable enclaves, trying to make sense of the revolution that did not happen. Clearly, we did not understand the worldview of the poor people who did not revolt when, according to our rationality, they should have. Very worrying to some was a realization that perhaps our cocooned world was in some danger.

The Davos version of corporate capitalism chafed at the boundaries created by nations. It railed against the rules created by national governments to protect the interests of their citizens. Economists calculated the costs to GDP growth created by these rules. Some, taking a long view of history, declared that the idea of countries with sovereign governments had become an anachronism. The drive for GDP growth and advances of communication technologies would break down national barriers, they hoped.

However, other longue durée forces of history are creating the need for stronger and better national governments. The first is that people want to choose their own government and make it accountable to them. Therefore, there is a trend towards more localization of governments—from Europe to countries in Europe (as in Brexit), and within European countries (Scotland). In India too, the trend is towards empowering governments in states and cities.

The second trend is an increasing consciousness of 'identities' and national histories. In a rootless world of global economics, people seek psychological stability and continuity of their history. They reach out for tribal camaraderie within their own people. Thus, the Soviet Union and Yugoslavia broke up into countries that formed around earlier histories. When people feel the established system is unfair to them, they will unite with others like themselves to fight for their rights, as the black Americans seem to be doing yet again in the US, and Kashmiris in India.

The third trend is the use of violence by disaffected people to terrorize the system. Modern technologies can enable 'anyone, from anywhere, to strike anywhere', as Donald Rumsfeld, the then US Defence Secretary had said after 9/11. Citizens have become fearful and are demanding their governments to provide them security against such random violence. Therefore, governments are strengthening their systems of surveillance, and use these same technologies, that empower citizens, to snoop on them. Although people complain that their government has become a 'Big Brother' invading citizens' privacies, they also want a stronger and better government in their country for their own security.

When the Berlin Wall was pulled down 28 years ago, some believed the history of ideological conflicts had ended. That illusion continued very briefly until the end of the millennium. Then history returned with a vengeance. The economics of globalization had failed to flatten the primal forces of tribalism, nativism and cultural identities. Civilizations clashed. A war was declared against terrorism. Geopolitics has returned with the resurgence of Russian nationalism and the rise of China.

National boundaries and national governments may be a problem for smooth global economics. But people need national governments to meet their other fundamental demands of self-determination and security.

OUR HISTORY, OUR IDENTITY

The French Revolution of 1789 propagated the revolutionary

idea, in Wallerstein's words, 'that "sovereignty"—the right of the state to make autonomous decisions within its realm—did not reside in (belong to) either a monarch or a legislature but in the "people" who, alone, could legitimate a regime.'[4] This new way of thinking about processes of political and social change leads to questions about the identity of 'we the people', and the agents of change, and how we the people form our shared identity.

People can be rallied together by invoking pride in their collective identity. One morning, on the forest path in Mashobra, I met two local men. I asked them about their lives. They seemed happy. Those days, the Indian media was filled with evaluations of the Narendra Modi-led government, which had completed two years in office. I asked the two about their thoughts of the government's performance so far. Both replied that while their families had been staunch Congress supporters for generations, and they had voted for the Congress in the last national election, they felt proud as Indians whenever they heard that the peripatetic Prime Minister Modi was making a good impression on people in other countries.

India is often described as an 'incredible' country on account of its diversity—diversity of religions, races, languages and geographies within it; as well as the rich history that has coursed through it, over thousands of years. This incredible complexity would make it difficult for anyone to define a singular idea of India. Incredible in its diversity, India has huge

---

[4]Wallerstein, Immanuel, *World-Systems Analysis*, Duke University Press, 2004, pp 237.

challenges before it, of creating good livelihoods and jobs for millions of people, improving their health and education, and lifting them sustainably out of poverty. Systems function well when their components are aligned. They become dysfunctional when coordination amongst the components breaks down. For India to progress faster to fulfil the needs of its citizens, Indians must overcome many internal differences. They must collaborate to shape their collective future. India's energetic democracy is often blamed for the Indian State's inability to get things done faster. Some even say that India would have grown much faster if dictatorship had preceded democracy. While dictatorships have not always produced well-run states, efficient institutions of the state are functioning well in many Western democracies. Political scientists, such as Francis Fukuyama (*Political Order and Political Decay: From the Industrial Revolution to the Globalization of Democracy*)[5] and Daron Acemoglu (*Why Nations Fail: The Origins of Power, Prosperity, and Poverty*),[6] maintain that strong state institutions are necessary for sustainable growth, regardless of whether they are produced by democracy or dictatorship.

Political scientists, including Fukuyama and Michael Cook (*Ancient Religions, Modern Politics: The Islamic Case in Comparative Perspective*), point out that the formation of strong States has often been enabled by the forging of a strong

---

[5]Fukuyama, Francis, *Political Order and Political Decay: From the Industrial Revolution to the Globalization of Democracy*, Farrar, Straus and Giroux, 2014.
[6]Acemoglu, Daron, *Why Nations Fail: The Origins of Power, Prosperity, and Poverty*, Pbk, Ed., Crown Business, 2013.

national identity, which has frequently been based on ethnicity or religion.[7] Germany, Japan, Korea, Singapore, France after the Revolution and even Israel are some examples of this. Therefore, it is tempting to conclude that Indians must be rallied around a shared national identity to enable the building of a strong State that can impose order and get things done. However, a special challenge that India has if it follows this route, as Cook explains, is that there is no ethnicity or religion that can rally all Indians into one nation.

Aryan culture cannot be India's identity. Dravidians in the South have made it clear that they were settled on India's land before the Aryans even arrived, and they are proud of their ancient, well-evolved culture and languages. To the East, other ethnic groups resent being treated as second-class Indian citizens. Religion also cannot unify all Indians, though India proudly has almost all the religions of the world. The religion of the majority, Hinduism, with its caste system, has been unable to contain everyone equally even within itself. Moreover, the beauty of Hinduism is that it accepts the fact that people can have many beliefs and many ways to their gods. The imposition of any singular version of Hinduism may even divide Hindus rather than unite the whole country.

Outside my Mashobra apartment, a new neighbour introduced himself to me one evening. He had also come to the hills to escape Delhi's summer heat. He had recently retired

---

[7]Cook, Michael, *Ancient Religions, Modern Politics: The Islamic Case in Comparative Perspective*, Princeton University Press, 2014.

as a director of a large company. He seemed 'people like us'. I asked him about his post-retirement plans. He said he planned to write a book on 'What is wrong with Muslims'. The shock in my eyes, which I could not hide, prompted him to explain that his parents had been refugees from Pakistan, which he wrongly believed, was enough to make him an authority on Muslims. My parents had been refugees from Pakistan too. But I have other views.

India's history is a composition of many histories. Any attempt to impose a single vision of India's history is a fool's game. It will create divisions within people, as evident from the recent efforts to rewrite Indian history. A shared, aspirational vision of what India must become is necessary to align the energies of all Indians in shaping their future. A foundational element of this vision of India has to be that India is a conglomeration of many diverse people with different histories. Ultimately, the idea of India must be what a billion Indians think it is. All of them will not see India in the same way. Their lenses are shaped by their personal histories. Yet all must respect other Indians as being just as much Indian as themselves.

A strong Indian State must be formed around a vision of the future, as the US was, and not around a religion and selective history. India's Prime Minister says that the Constitution is his God. For all Indians too, their Constitution must be the guide to the conduct of the State, and not their version of India's history.

While all Indians cannot have the same lenses, they must acknowledge that other Indians also have a right to their perspectives of India. Despite these different lenses, there must be something common in their views of India for it to become their collective vision of *our* India. Indians must discover the highest common factors in their multiple perspectives and aspirations. Therefore, whatever be India's past, those within India's present borders must listen to each other deeply to understand who *we* are, and to shape *our* future together.

The central question of our times is, 'How on Earth can we live together?' How can we Indians live harmoniously together, and with our Mother Earth? How can people of all countries live harmoniously together and with their one shared Earth?

Listening to others is not easy when what they say seems so wrong. It may seem wrong because others see the same reality through different lenses. Like the blind men around the elephant, each of us is convinced that what we see is the truth, which it may be. But it is not the whole truth.

WHOSE SIDE AM I ON?

2

WE ARE NOT LISTENING

It is the disease of not listening, the malady of not marking, that I am troubled withal.

—William Shakespeare, *Henry IV Part 2*

In the summer of 2011, when India was preparing its 12th Five Year Plan (which turned out to be its last one because the Planning Commission was closed sine die in 2014), the Principal Secretary for Labour and Employment in the Government of Maharashtra asked me to chair a meeting of heads of labour unions and industry associations in Mumbai.

I had been appointed a Member of the Planning Commission in 2009 by the then Prime Minister, Dr Manmohan Singh, who is widely acclaimed as the father of India's path-breaking pro-market reforms in 1991. He had asked me to prepare a plan for creating more industry, manufacturing and jobs in the country. Indian industry had been stifled by a rigidly controlled system of industrial licencing until the late 1980s. Bureaucrats in Delhi determined what had to be produced, who would be permitted to produce it, and how much of it they could produce. There was a huge pent-up demand for many things but insufficient production and limited options. For example, only two makes of cars were available, and even though they were of shoddy quality, customers waited for many years to get an allotment because they had no other choice. Telephone connections from the government controlled monopoly and took many years to materialize, with a lot of palm greasing required to expedite them a bit.

The 1991 reforms abolished the system of industrial licencing. Investors and producers became free to meet the pent-up demands. International trade was thrown open. Foreign-made goods, which Indian consumers had been yearning for, began to flow in. Many models of TVs, electronic goods, home appliances and cars, produced in Japan, Korea, Europe and the US, were now on offer. Indian consumers had never had it so good. From their perspective, the economic reforms were a great success.

The overall economy grew well in the years following the economic reforms. However, the growth was fuelled by a remarkable growth of the service sector and not manufacturing. There was speculation that India may have leap-frogged the historical growth pattern of developing economies, which transitioned from a dominance of the agricultural sector to growth of labour-intensive manufacturing to absorb labour displaced by improvements in productivity in agriculture, and only then to expansion of the services sector as manufacturing productivity also improved. China, the other billion population developing economy, had followed the historical pattern, and had become the factory of the world and, consequently, had achieved a remarkable reduction in poverty.

India's manufacturing sector, which had contributed to about 16 per cent of India's GDP in 1991, remained moribund, despite growth and reforms, whose principal thrust was to release the brakes and remove controls on the growth of India's industrial and manufacturing sectors. This had resulted in a slower growth of jobs and employment in spite of high overall growth. There was a great concern that India was beginning to experience 'jobless growth', the implications of which had begun to worry the PM and India's economic policy-makers. India had the largest population of young persons (under 30 years old) in the world that, according to economists, would provide the Indian economy with a 'demographic dividend'. However, for these young persons to contribute to the demographic dividend, they must be employed and earn incomes. Otherwise, by their underemployment, and their inability to acquire the consumer goodies that were becoming available to Indian citizens with the opening up of the economy, and to which they aspired, their dissatisfactions could lead to a demographic disaster. Indeed, signals of an impending disaster were appearing in various parts of the country, with unemployed youth participating in political protest movements, some turning violent.

India needed to create more jobs. Indian policy-makers would have to go back to the drawing board, to understand the factors crimping the growth of India's manufacturing sector. The PM expected me to understand the constraints on growth of the manufacturing sector from its stakeholders. Amongst these constraints, a principal one, according to investors and employers, was the tangle of Indian labour laws. There were too many, several were antiquated and generally badly administered, with government inspectors harassing employers, especially small entrepreneurs. Therefore, employers were reluctant to employ more people and invest in the growth of their enterprises. They demanded a greater freedom to 'hire and fire', which, they said, would encourage them to take risks by investing more in their enterprises.

The unions also demanded improvements in the administration of labour laws. They insisted that the laws did not provide sufficient social security to employees, which would become even more necessary if employers were to be given more freedom to hire and fire employees. Moreover, they complained, employers were circumventing the laws, by hiring workers through labour contractors, and were not providing these workers with fair wages, statutory benefits and even the required safety equipment in many cases.

There was a stand-off between unions and employers in reforming the labour laws. The government was unable to get them to agree. The Indian states have a large, constitutionally granted role in the framing of and the administration of labour laws. As the largest manufacturing state in India, Maharashtra was expected to play a leading role in the reframing of labour laws. Hence, the state's Principal Secretary for Labour and Employment, Dr Kavita Gupta, invited me to chair a meeting between the heads of labour unions and industry associations to agree to an agenda for the reforms.

THE MEETING

I arrived early for the meeting before all participants. Dr Gupta took me into the meeting room and sat with me at the head of a long, large conference table. There she briefed me about who she anticipated would attend the meeting. She expected about a dozen representatives each from unions and industry associations. She knew them and had met them in many meetings, both separately and together.

I asked her about her expectations from the meeting. She said she wanted them to support some changes that she sought to make to improve the effectiveness of labour regulations. I then asked her about her thoughts on my role in the meeting. She said I was a very senior person in the Central government—at the level of a minister of state and the participants were keen to hear my views. I should convey that the government was very sincere in bringing about reforms in labour regulations. I should also urge the unions and industrialists to work together to improve industrial relations so that the economy could grow faster. 'Say the same blasé things that senior government officials say,' I thought to myself. 'They must have heard these platitudes hundreds of times.'

The participants entered the room soon afterwards through the single door opposite the head of the table. As they came in, the union representatives were ushered towards one side of the table and the industry representatives to the other. Participants on each side shook hands with each other, and some even hugged each other warmly. They smiled and waved politely at participants on the other side. The setting of the room had already divided the participants into two sides.

Dr Gupta commenced the meeting with a welcome to all and especially to me. She said the agenda was to obtain stakeholders' support for the improvements being made by the labour department, and to discuss wider cooperation amongst stakeholders and the government. She had invited me to chair the discussions. She asked the participants to introduce themselves and make very brief opening comments if they wished to.

The union side went first. Some spoke very briefly, others longer. Then the industry representatives spoke. Since they were going second, some of them reacted to statements made from the union side, which provoked some union leaders to respond. Very soon, mere introductions were in danger of slipping into a tense debate even before the meeting could get to its stated agenda.

I had been taking notes of the names and what each person had said. The introductions had gone around the room from Dr Gupta on my left, and had come back to me from the other side. It seemed it was my turn to say something and Dr Gupta asked me if I had any opening remarks to make.

I turned to the union side and said, 'I have heard and noted what you have said. I want to ask you how many times before this meeting have you said the same things to industry representatives at other meetings?' The answer was, 'A hundred times! We keep saying these things but "they" do not hear us!' Then I asked the industry side the same question. The answer was the same, 'A hundred times, but "they" are unwilling to hear us!'

I posed a question to all. 'What then have you achieved by saying the same things yet again if you are not being heard?' 'Moreover', I said, 'I don't think you have really listened to what others are saying. Let me read from my notes of what I have heard so far.'

I pointed out that amongst rhetorical flourishes from some on the union side about exploitation of labour; there were other serious comments too. For example, some union leaders had said that industries in India must become competitive with foreign producers so that jobs would be created in the country. Some had said that employers must invest in their employees' skills and welfare so as to improve the productivity of the workforce.

From the employers' side, I had heard some say that unions were only interested in protecting the high wages and job security of their own union members. Whereas, I pointed out, many union leaders were talking about the need to improve working conditions and wages of casual workers who were not members of their unions. I pointed out to the union side's observations made by some on the employers' side about the need for better cooperation amongst employers and unions to improve productivity and skill levels.

As I narrated what I had heard each side say, I noticed something quite interesting. When I mentioned that the unions were not focused on their own members only, contrary to the widespread view, some industry participants looked alarmed. 'Whose side was I on?' they seemed to question. When I said that many industry participants seemed genuinely interested in the welfare of all their workers, some union leaders, it seemed to me, silently said to themselves, 'We knew he was always on the side of industries.' The question was—*whose side was I on?*

THE FOG OF MISPERCEPTIONS

I concluded my remarks by saying that there was a lot of common ground that had already been expressed, which I hoped we would build upon. Unfortunately, it was hidden by a fog of misperceptions about the 'other' side. I hoped we would not continue to see merely stereotypes of the other side. I urged everyone to take off the filters in their minds that made them hear only what they expected to hear; and instead listen to what was actually said. Only then would we make any progress towards the 'win-win' solutions that we glibly say we must find. And, if we do not listen deeply to the other side, and continue to only find affirmation about what we assume the other side believes, we would remain stuck in a dead-end discourse. We would have left after yet another meeting in which we would have said what we have always said and complained about not being heard.

The situation was similar to an old story about a kingdom that was lost for want of a nail in the shoe of a horse. Because a nail was missing, the horseshoe dropped. Because the shoe dropped, the horse could not run. Because the horse could not run, the messenger could not deliver the warning to the king. Because the warning was not delivered, the king was not prepared and the battle was lost. Because the battle was lost, the kingdom was lost. Something as simple and small as a badly fixed nail resulted in catastrophic consequences.

For over 25 years, both unions and employers have been demanding reforms of India's labour laws. Both sides insist many laws are archaic and are badly implemented. The government has, rather unsuccessfully, tried to bring them together repeatedly in tripartite meetings to reform laws. Meanwhile, industry has not been growing sufficiently and not enough jobs are being created. With something as small as deeper listening to what is behind the stereotypes in their respective minds, a handful of union leaders and employers could begin a movement of reform that could impact the lives of hundreds of millions of Indians.

A few weeks after the meeting in Mumbai, I was approached by the President of the Employers' Federation of India, Rajeev Dubey, and the Chairman of the Confederation of Indian Industry's National Council for Industrial Relations, Surinder Kapur. They had been meeting with union leaders for a year and had noted a willingness in some of them to work with industry for reforms. At the same time, they had noted unwillingness amongst many industry leaders to engage in a dialogue with unions. Since I was the member incharge of industry, Rajeev and Surinder requested me to convene a meeting of leaders of the principal industry associations to moot the need for a new dialogue with unions. They also asked me to invite some union leaders who would be amenable to a new dialogue. I met Vrijesh Upadhyay, the General Secretary of the Bharti Mazdur Sangh (BMS), the largest national union. He liked the idea and agreed to ask a few other union leaders.

We agreed that the meeting would be informal and exploratory without any pre-determined agenda. The participants would deliberate on what they should do together. Both sides said that I would have to play two roles to give the process a good start. One was to convene the meeting in the Planning Commission, as they believed that invitees were more likely to attend if they were invited by a member of the Commission. The other was a request to facilitate the discussions amongst them. I agreed.

The problem of convening the meeting in the Planning Commission was that there was no suitable room for the sort of meeting I envisaged—a dialogue directly between unions and employers, and not a typical meeting convened by a senior government official. In the latter kind, the usual form is for everyone to address the official in the few minutes that each participant is given to speak. But the objective of this meeting was for participants to speak to each other and not to me.

There were many meeting rooms in the Planning Commission. Some were set up with huge tables in the middle, around which people would sit in long rows of chairs. These rooms were too big and too formal for the informality required for the small, ice-breaking meeting between a dozen or so leaders of unions and employers. Other meeting rooms had narrow tables set up in a U-format. At the deep end of that U was a high chair for the senior official conducting the meeting with chairs alongside for other senior persons. The participants would invariably sit along the arms of the U with others like themselves, as the union leaders and employers had in Mumbai, to identify which side they were on. This arrangement was also not suitable for the meeting I had in mind.

We had no choice so we met in a room with the U-format, except that I did not sit on the high chair in the middle. I sat on a chair at the end of one of arms of the U, furthest from the centre where the least important person in a meeting would be expected to sit. The advantage of this chair was that I could walk into the U whenever I wanted to, and walk up to any of the participants, just as Joe Curry had done in the transformative meeting of the Telco managers 50 years ago.

When the participants came in, they were unsettled by the arrangement. They asked me to move to the high chair. I explained why I was sitting where I was, and suggested that any one of them could take the high chair treating it as any other chair. They found this very difficult to do. It remained empty for a while, till someone pushed it aside and replaced it with another chair like every other.

I reminded everyone that they had asked me to facilitate a meeting amongst them and I intended to do just that. I said I would not be the chairman of the meeting to arbitrate between the parties or to give decisions. However, I would be incharge of the quality of their deliberations. If I felt someone had not listened to another, I would intercede. 'We would have an "un-conference" in a conventional conference room,' I said. It would be a meeting with a difference, they agreed.

That meeting began a process of deep listening and of building trust between union leaders and employers, the progress of which I will report in the later chapters of this book. In those chapters, we will examine the layouts of meeting places, as well as the principles of conducting meetings that enable people to listen to each other more carefully. This will ensure that, metaphorically, the loose nail is hammered back into the horseshoe and the message is not lost.

3

LISTENING TO PEOPLE NOT LIKE US

The golden rule of conduct, therefore, is mutual toleration, seeing that we will never all think alike and we shall always see Truth in fragment and from different angles of vision.

—Mahatma Gandhi

For some years now, I have been observing in many meetings how little the participants listen to each other. They seem unable, and even unwilling to pay attention to others, especially when the subject is contentious and when there is a greater need for people to understand each other's points of view—like the discussion about labour reforms.

For example, when an international consulting organization tried to convene a meeting of stakeholders to examine the reasons for persistent malnutrition of children in India, some health activists refused to attend if executives of multinational companies (MNCs) producing pharmaceutical products would be present at the meeting. The MNCs were also reluctant to meet with the activists who, they said, had made up their minds

IT IS ONE WORLD AFTER ALL

that MNCs were only interested in making more money rather than improving health.

After the flash floods that devastated Mumbai in 2005, I was asked by the Confederation of Indian Industry (CII) to facilitate a meeting to discuss improvements of the city's infrastructure. I asked all key stakeholders to be included and drew up a list which included a slum dwellers' association and some environmental groups. Some of the industry leaders balked. 'Why would we have them in the meeting? We know their views. They are the cause of problems in the improvement of the city,' they said. The slum dwellers' association and environmental groups also saw no point in meeting the industry leaders. 'They have their own views and have made up their minds about what is required. They are unwilling to consider anything else,' they complained.

As with the unions and employers, these groups had also made up their minds about the 'other side'. If they met again, they would attack each other again, and not listen to each other. Thus, problems that could be solved only by listening to each other and combining perspectives have become chronic.

The mandate of India's Planning Commission, in which I served as a member for five years, was the planning of inclusive, sustainable and faster growth of the Indian economy. Most large and complex problems, such as economic growth, social development, urban improvement and public health, have many facets to them. They require many perspectives to be combined for their resolution. Within the Planning Commission were several experts—economists, sociologists, scientists, and experts in education, healthcare and many other subjects. They operated within organizational silos and within their own 'intellectually gated communities'. Observing meetings amongst them, I noted their competitiveness, and their motivation to show their own side (their department, their discipline) as superior, and their drive to prove that the other side was deficient and wrong. The casualty, sadly, was listening to others' points of view and, with that, the progress of the country.

Whenever the Planning Commission organized public consultations amongst stakeholders on health, education, urban development and many other complex issues, the animosity and deep divisions amongst the stakeholders was very evident. Social activists and corporate executives were generally at logger heads with each other. 'Neo-liberal' economists and 'socialist' economists were viscerally opposed. Those who believed that large scale organizations are essential for efficiency and impact, dismissed proponents of grass roots community-based organizations as foolish idealists.

During my tenure, there was growing demand from the states and civil society organizations (CSOs) for the Planning Commission's consultations to be less formal and more inclusive. Many CSOs came together on a common platform called *Wada Na Todo Abhiyan* (WNTA) to demand more people's participation in the planning process. *Wada Na Todo Abhiyan* translates into—'Do not break your promise campaign'. They wanted the Planning Commission to be accountable for the promises made in its plans, and wanted it to live up to its promise, in its charter, to associate with people and obtain their cooperation.

WNTA knocked on the doors of the Planning Commission in 2011 when it was time to formulate the Approach to the 12th Five Year Plan. My fellow member of the Planning Commission, Dr Syeda Hameed, and I met them and arrived at an agreement about possible collaborations between the Planning Commission and WNTA to bring in the voices of the most excluded and marginalized people so as to make the approach more inclusive.

The WNTA welcomed this move and made the following observations in Approaching Equity: Civil Society Inputs for the Approach Paper—12th Five Year Plan.[8]

The Planning Commission has, in a path-breaking move, approached civil society organizations to engage with them openly, formally and systematically, and opened up the process for inputs into the approach paper (instead of sharing and seeking inputs after the draft approach is ready). Civil society groups feel this move is a key window of opportunity to actualize the shift of the planning process to a people-led one, make the 12th Five Year Plan inclusive, and create spaces for the most marginalized. There is also a need to institutionalize this process into a formal, systemic one.

Both the Planning Commission and WNTA were keen to make the consultation process systematic and mutually satisfying. WNTA insisted that hundreds of CSOs would be willing to participate if the process was more serious and

---

[8]http://www.undp.org/content/dam/india/docs/approaching_equity_civil_society_inputs_for_the_approach_paper_12th_five-year_plan.pdf

better designed than the previous engagements of the Planning Commission.[9]

How do you listen to hundreds of CSOs representing a variety of issues and diverse groups of citizens spread around the country? Further, this had to be accomplished in a short time since the Approach paper had to be completed within three months. WNTA suggested that the consultation process would be much sharper if the Commission was clear about the questions it wanted to consult the CSOs on. Fortunately, the Commission was ready with twelve questions.

A meeting was convened of the WNTA leaders with the members of the Commission to design the consultation process. The list of questions elicited a favourable response with some WNTA leaders offering answers there and then. I asked them to pause, as the meeting was convened to design a consultative mechanism and not to discuss the answers. I insisted that we wanted to hear people's views.

The person I had interrupted was offended. He claimed that his CSO represented over a million people, whose opinions he knew well. When I asked how often the members of the CSO met, he insisted that they met all the time. I could sense the outrage building within him. How dare I doubt his credibility? But I pushed on. If the organization was having meetings

---

[9] WNTA has recorded the names of 600 organizations and another 200 civil society experts who participated in the process that followed. The Planning Commission noted that another 200 organizations were also consulted in addition to those who came on the WNTA platform. Thus, the total numbers approached 1,000.

frequently, it would be easy for it to include discussions of the Commission's questions in meetings over the next few weeks. I wondered if he would consider that. The riposte to that was quite swift. Would I or some other members of the Commission come to the meetings? Surely it would be of more use for us to hear the people's views, than for him and the other leaders of his CSO, since they were already people's views.

From this repartee emerged the need for all the CSOs to make their own processes systematic. It also impelled them to prepare their calendars of meetings in which they would discuss the questions with their members with a view to enable members of the Commission to participate in some of them. A date was set by which the Commission was to receive the submissions from the CSOs so that their suggestions could be considered before finalization of the draft Approach paper.

The members of the Commission particularly wanted to listen to the views of the citizen groups that were the most excluded from the mainstream, such as the Dalits, tribal minorities, women, children and the differently abled. There were many CSOs representing each of these groups of citizens. The members requested that the submissions from each of these groups be consolidated by WNTA. A leader of a large CSO said that her organization would prefer to submit its recommendations directly, and that other CSOs could do the same. That way the Commission would have the benefit of many views, she suggested.

Thinking ahead, I wondered how the Planning Commission would consolidate the views of all CSOs representing women, for example. What if the views of organizations who knew the needs of women very well, as they claimed, were not aligned? On what basis would the Planning Commission make a judgement of a better option for women? If the Planning Commission was inclined to go with one view and not another, it could be blamed for taking sides. And if the Planning Commission settled on a compromise which neither liked, both would accuse it of not understanding what was best for women!

My suggestion that the CSOs should thrash out their disagreements amongst themselves was received with some mirth. 'Which world do you live in, Mr Maira? Do you know how difficult it is for two CSOs with different ideologies, who have publicly disagreed, to agree with each other?' I persisted that the women of India would be served best if those who knew their needs could come to an agreement amongst themselves. It was the same for the other CSOs representing other citizen groups.

Later, when the Approach paper was published after all consultations, WNTA's leaders met with the Planning Commission to do an 'after action review'. They provided feedback on ways to improve the process in future. They said that the Commission's most valuable contribution was to insist that the CSOs learn to listen to each other and find solutions together. It was, by far, the best way in which the CSOs could serve their stakeholders.

However, the CSOs were very disappointed with the Planning Commission's draft of the Approach paper, as they could not see their points of view incorporated in it. It seemed to them that the Planning Commission had not heard them at all.

LISTENING TO PEOPLE NOT LIKE US

They requested a formal meeting with the Deputy Chairman of the Planning Commission to convey their disappointment and also make another effort to get their points of view understood.

The Deputy Chairman heard them and explained that the Planning Commission was not obliged to accept everything the CSOs proposed. The Planning Commission had to consider the views of others too, who were often not in agreement with the views of CSOs, and then make up its own mind about the best course of action for the country. Some CSOs alleged that the Planning Commission had a pro-Western and pro-business bias and was 'anti-people'. Others quietened down these shrill protestors, and supported the Deputy Chairman's position that the Planning Commission had to consider many points of view. However, they would have liked the Approach paper to present the principal points of view and explain why it was recommending one view in the interests of the people.

Moreover, they said the language of the Approach paper was not easy for the CSOs and their members to understand. Could it not be made simpler? The Deputy Chairman's cursory response to this, which was that the Approach paper was not being written for the benefit of CSOs but was addressed to people who understood planning language, annoyed many of them. If the Planning Commission would not even admit the need to engage the people in a dialogue for which it would have to adopt a language they understood, there was no point in continuing the meeting. At this point, the Deputy Chairman left the meeting.

The leaders of WNTA who had arranged the meeting were dismayed. So was I. We had hoped to build better bridges between civil society and the Planning Commission. Now there was a break down. I offered to stay back and discuss with whomsoever from the CSOs would be willing to, how the process could be changed to achieve the objective for which WNTA and the Planning Commission had begun their innovative collaboration.

SCENARIO PLANNING

I suggested to the CSOs that we may consider using the 'scenario planning' process. Some of them had heard about the application of the process in South Africa in the 1990s, when the new government was sworn in after the abolition of the apartheid. The expectations of people in South Africa were very high. But so were the tensions within the country. A good process was required to analyse the country's development strategy, considering its economic, social and political challenges. This strategy would have to be understood and supported by citizens to create alignment amongst them, without which the country would tear apart.

The output of the process became known as the 'Mont Fleur scenarios' because the participants in the process met to reflect on the future of their country in a small hotel named Mont Fleur. The participants represented the contending stakeholders: the blacks and whites; and industry, civil society and labour unions. They invited Adam Kahane, a scenarist from the Shell Oil Company, which was a pioneer in the use of scenario planning in the corporate world, to guide them through this process. These leaders engaged in deep dialogue, and listened to each other's hopes and suggestions. They developed a systems map of the territory of change that South Africa would have to traverse and highlighted the alternative paths through it. They evaluated the risks and possibilities on these alternative paths.

These leaders, who were (and would remain) competitors to each other outside the process, had developed a shared view of the world of which they were all a part. If in their eagerness to win their internal competition, they were to destroy their world, the victory would be not worth anything, even to the victor. They realized that they would have to convey this view to their supporters too in a language that the people could understand. What better language than pictures and metaphors?

Therefore, they created memorable pictures of the plausible future for South Africa and laid out the choices before the country. Each of these scenarios was supported by a simple systems' analysis that explained the forces that would cause that scenario to emerge. The desirable scenario was called 'The Flight of the Flamingos', in which the contending parties would squawk at each other for a little while, and then would slowly take off together in formation. It was another image of the vision of the 'rainbow nation' that President Mandela evoked so powerfully to inspire cooperation. (The other less desirable scenarios were called 'Lame Duck', 'Ostrich' and 'Icarus'.)

Several people in the meeting of the CSOs with the Planning Commission volunteered to participate in a scenario planning exercise to shape strategies for the country's development, if I were to organize it. Indian business leaders also volunteered to join in, as did leaders of Indian think-tanks engaged on strategic, trade and environmental issues. Together, they used the tools of systems thinking and scenario planning to shape strategies for India's progress. The India scenarios were included by the Planning Commission in the 12th Five Year Plan for the country under the following titles: 'The Flotilla Advances', 'Muddling Along' and 'Falling Apart'.[10]

The participants in the process maintained that Muddling Along was the scenario of India in which stakeholders were unable to come to any agreement. It was close to the present condition of the country, they felt. Their fear was that divisive forces could make the stakeholders fall apart further, and the country's progress would be retarded. Therefore, unless there was a concerted effort with stronger and more effective processes of democratic deliberation for stakeholders to form themselves into a flotilla that advances together towards a shared vision, the scenario of Muddling Along could deteriorate into a worse scenario of Falling Apart.

ADDRESSING INTRACTABLE GLOBAL PROBLEMS

Complex and systemic issues such as climate change, persistent poverty, increasing inequality within and across countries, and

---

[10] The India scenarios may be accessed on the former Planning Commission's website, as well as in my book *An Upstart in Government: Journeys of Change and Learning* (Rupa Publications, 2015).

increasing terrorism and violence, have many facets to them and no easy solutions. They must be seen from many points of view and require many perspectives to be combined to understand their root causes. Diverse people must be willing, and able to listen to each other to implement sustainable solutions to them. There is an increasing gap between, on one hand, a need for deeper listening across the many boundaries of ideology, culture and intellectual disciplines that divide us, and our abilities to listen to each other on the other hand. This does not bode well for the future of human civilization.

The liberal democratic order is imperilled. Democratic institutions have become diseased. The democratic body seems unable to cope with challenges of disunity and differences amongst peoples, across countries and within countries. Social media is a new virus complicating deeper causes of ill-health. Brexit and the startling outcome of the 2016 US presidential elections, like a severe chest pain, were warnings that all is not well within the democratic body. Signs of disease are appearing in many democracies, in Europe, Asia, and elsewhere.

Examples of poor listening when people with different beliefs are brought together are ubiquitous. Debates on TV are deliberately set up as gladiatorial fights between opponents for the entertainment of viewers. The participants do not listen to each other. They only want to make their own points and win the debate. In social media, it seems impossible to have any dialogue in which participants will listen to others with different points of view. They are all locked within their own communities of people they 'like' and 'follow'. They only lob epithets across the walls at those on the other side.

Along with the decline of deep listening in public spaces, the ability to listen to others is also disappearing from private spaces with the spread of smartphones and social media. In her book *Reclaiming Conversation: The Power of Talk in a Digital Age* (Penguin Press, 2015), Shirley Turkle, who had been an enthusiast for the promise of digital technology, reports a troubling consequence:

> At work, at home, in politics and in love, we have sacrificed conversation for mere connection. At the dinner table, children compete with smartphones for their parents' attention. At work, we retreat to our screens, forgoing the water-cooler conversation that once made us productive and engaged. We share opinions online that our friends will agree with, avoiding the real conflicts and solutions of the public square. When we turn to our devices instead of to one another, the cost is high: a loss of empathy. So it is not surprising that in the past twenty years, we've seen a 40 per cent decline in the markers for empathy among college students, most of it within the past ten years. It is a trend that researchers link to the new presence of digital communications.

Why have we not noted the consequences of the decline in our collective abilities to listen to each other? Have we even noticed that we are not listening to each other?

A few authors have been pointing to the decline in the quality of public discourse and its effects on the quality of politics and society. These include Deborah Tannen in *The Argument Culture: Stopping America's War of Words* (Ballentine Publishing Company, 1998); Lewis H. Lapham in *Gag Rule: On the Suppression of Dissent and the Stifling of Democracy* (Penguin Books, 2004); and Shirley Turkle (ibid). However, an awareness of the poor and declining quality of public and private discourse has hardly received any attention compared with the floodlights of attention on advances of globalization and technology. This is despite the fact that the effect of the deterioration in abilities of people to listen to each other deeply may have as much (or perhaps even greater) effect on the future of humanity.

The parable of the frog in a jar of water, the temperature of which is rising slowly, may provide an explanation. The frog does not realize that the temperature is increasing because it is rising slowly and he adjusts himself to it, until it becomes too hot for his body to bear, and he dies. However, if he is lucky, there may be a sharp spike in the rising temperature, which shakes him out of his complacency and he jumps out and survives.

Could the shocks of Brexit in the UK, and the election of Donald Trump as President of the US, wake us up to realize that even in the most open societies, with great freedom of speech and widely accessible social media, like the UK and the US, people have not been really listening to the concerns of others within their own countries? Also, the dawning realization that social media is not the panacea that it was expected to be to bring all people together, and that it is indeed aggravating the problem of divisiveness, should wake us up. We must examine the fundamental requirements for good dialogue amongst people with differences in which they are willing and able to listen to each other.

Just as many organs must be healthy for a human body to be healthy, many institutions must also function well and together for a democracy to be robust. Somethings as simple as sounds and deep breathing are a tonic for improving bodily (and mental) health: this is the wisdom of yoga. Similarly, something as simple and fundamental as deep listening to others can be a tonic for improving the quality of democratic institutions.

4

WHY IS IT SO DIFFICULT TO LISTEN TO PEOPLE NOT LIKE US?

Where the world has not been broken up into fragments by narrow domestic walls;
Into that heaven of freedom, my Father, let my country awake.

—Rabindranath Tagore, *Gitanjali*

Why are people unable and unwilling to listen to each other, when by understanding each other and finding solutions together they could improve the world for everyone?

Our ability to listen is guided by and also impeded by structures in our minds. These structures are like the walls, doors and windows of a house that facilitate the lives and activities of the occupants of the house. The structures create order. They create spaces for cooking, washing and sanitary needs, and spaces for sleeping, sitting and eating. The doors and windows can be opened to let in people, wind and light, or be shut to keep them out. The structures of the house direct and impede our movements. Nevertheless, it is more comfortable

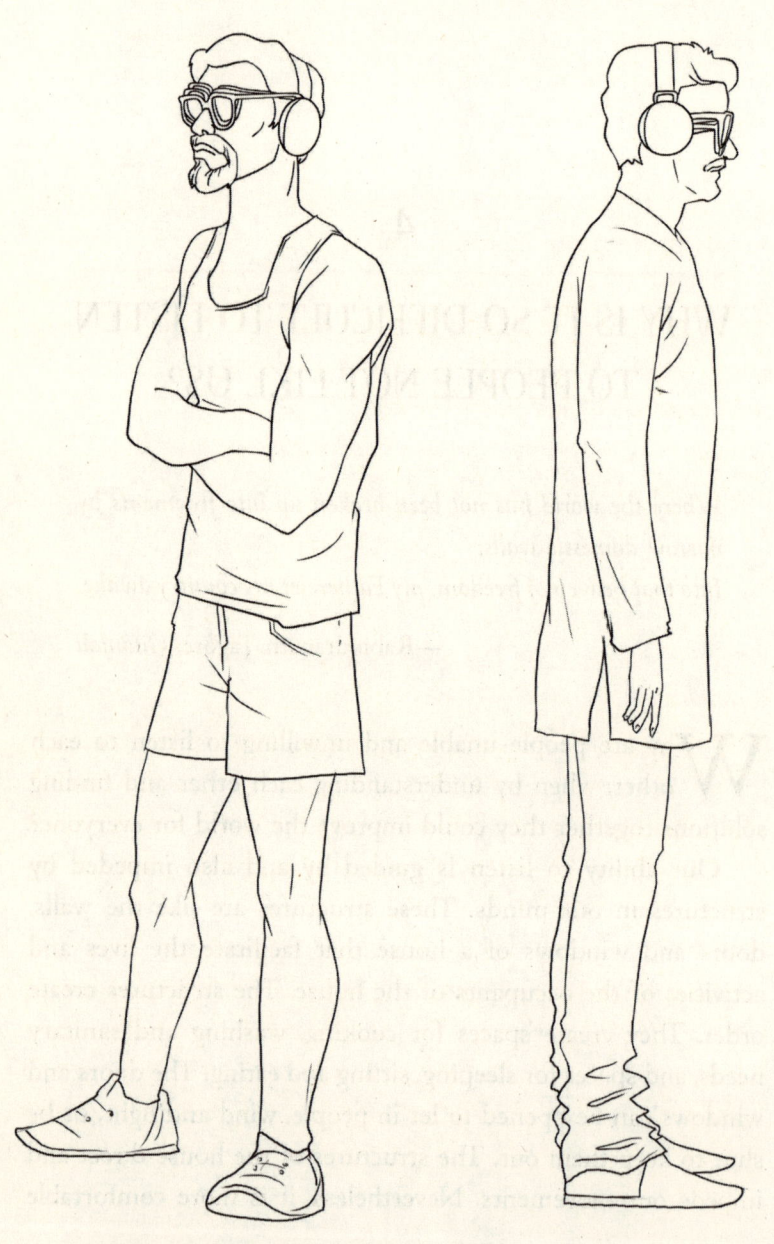

FILTERING OUT WHAT WE DO NOT WANT TO SEE OR HEAR

and safer to live in a house with structures than it is to live completely in the open.

Like the structures of a house that make living more efficient, the structures of our thoughts and of meetings make our listening more efficient. They influence our willingness and ability to listen. These structures are not 'concrete' like the structures of a house. They are invisible to us, yet they impede and direct our listening. Let us consider the forms of two structures that affect our ability to listen: structures of conversations and meetings; and structures of our thoughts.

STRUCTURES OF CONVERSATIONS AND SPACES FOR MEETINGS

Buildings serve many purposes and have many forms. If you were to ask an architect to design a building for you, he would immediately ask, 'What will be the purpose of the building?' Buildings can serve as a home, an office, a shopping complex, a hospital or an airport. Buildings for different purposes have different forms and different structures. The architect needs to know the purpose of the building so that he can give it the required form, and provide appropriate structures to enable the building to fulfil its purpose efficiently. The layouts of spaces and the locations of walls and openings must be different in a building that will be used as a home from a building that will be used as an office, and very different from a shopping complex or an airport!

Just as buildings serve many purposes, conversations and

meetings also serve many different purposes. Yet, we use the term 'meetings' very loosely. You say 'We had a meeting the other day', or 'We had a conversation, but it did not go well.' As an architect of meetings (and conversations), I would ask, 'What was the purpose of the meeting? Was it designed to fulfil its purpose?' Or, 'What was the nature of conversation you intended to have?'

Meetings and conversations for different purposes should take different forms and require different structures. A meeting between a suspect and an interrogator will be set up and run very differently to a meeting between two persons wanting to know each other. A meeting to determine which side is right and which side is wrong, as court proceedings are, must be very different to a meeting of inquiry in which many parties wish to understand a problem together.

Some of us from hot lands think of snow merely as a beautiful, undifferentiated white expanse to frolic in on a winter holiday. But Eskimos, who have to live amidst snow, must be able to discriminate different types of snow. They have 50 different words for snow to identify different types of snow, while most of us have only one word—snow. Similarly, though we know that meetings can have many forms and we often use different words, such as 'discussion', 'debate' and 'dialogue' to describe meetings, we use these words very loosely, without discrimination. We may say that two persons were in a 'dialogue' when they were actually having an adversarial 'debate'.

Meetings with the intention to enable people to listen deeply to each other, in other words to be a real dialogue, can degenerate into adversarial debates if they are not properly conducted. The format of the discussion between parties with different views distinguishes dialogues from debates and from other forms of discussion. Just as it will be difficult to make a cosy home in a building designed for an office, it is difficult to listen to others deeply in a meeting that is designed as a debate.

'Where do you stand in this matter?' We ask others, metaphorically, when we want to know what their views are. Where we sit in a meeting can define our place in the conversation: the roles we are expected to play, and which side we are supposed to be on. Where we sit vis-à-vis others also influences our perceptions of where they may stand in the matter.

Settings can be designed to fit the purpose of a meeting. Interrogators and clever negotiators understand how settings affect the dynamics amongst parties in a conversation. Persons who sit on a chair higher than others in a meeting appear more powerful and must be looked up to. They must be deferred to when they speak. Therefore, interrogators and cunning negotiators place themselves on a higher level physically, to make others look up to them and feel weaker in their presence. Interrogators position themselves with the glare of a window behind them so that the other person has to strain to read the expression on their face while they can look clearly into the other's eyes.

We will discuss structures of meetings further in Chapter 5.

STRUCTURES OF THOUGHT

All of us instinctively pay more attention to some things than to others. People everywhere get alarmed when they see a large fire or hear a loud explosion. Then there are other things that people react to differently. For example, some people would react with alarm to the sight of a man with a turban and beard, or a woman in a burqa, whereas to Muslims it is more likely to be a comforting sight. What we notice and how we react to it is conditioned by the collective experience of the communities to which we belong.

We are a part of many communities. At the broadest level, we belong to the community of Homo sapiens. All human beings are most likely to react with alarm at the sight of a bear: whereas a bear will have other feelings on seeing another bear. As human beings, we have many things in common which distinguish our views of the world from the views of other species.

We also belong to sub-sets of Homo sapiens, to communities with different histories, religions, customs and cultures. People within these communities can also have very different views of the state of the world around them. For instance, white Christian supporters of Donald Trump seem to see the world quite differently than other white Christian American citizens. They see the world through different 'lenses'. While some see progress in America, others see decline. Some see a system that provides opportunity to everyone; others see the system as unfair and rigged. They do not see 'eye to eye' at all.

WHY IS IT SO DIFFICULT TO LISTEN TO PEOPLE NOT LIKE US?

Differences of perceptions can go even further within broadly similar communities. Natural scientists, economists and anthropologists notice very different things in the same world around them. They wear different 'lenses' that make them focus on some facets of reality and filter out the other facets. Conversations amongst people from different disciplines are often not easy. They talk different languages. They live within different, intellectually gated communities.

In the words of the Noble laureate Rabindranath Tagore, we are living in 'a world broken into fragments by narrow domestic walls'. These walls, invisible to us, are the walls created in our minds by the different lenses through which we see the world. We find it difficult to listen to and understand others who see the world through different lenses. It is not at all easy to see our own lenses through which we see the world. It is also not easy to see what is going on in the backs of our heads.

Our lenses and habits of thought provide efficiency in our lives. They instinctively categorize and label what we see: what is good and what is bad, what is friendly and what is dangerous, who is 'with us' and who is 'against us'. We do not have to think about these things deeply: we can instantly react and act based on our superficial perceptions. We stay within our walls of safety and comfort. We do not listen to the real human being who is behind the stereotype we have in our minds.

Our lenses and our habits of thought make us unable and, often, unwilling to listen to others. They are not easy to change. But awareness of them will empower us. It will make us understand our own limitations, and to make allowances for these when we have conversations with others. Awareness will enable us to listen to what is going on in our own minds when we are listening to others. Thus, by listening deeply to others, not only will we understand others better, we can also understand ourselves better.

In Chapter 6, we will look into the different types of lenses we wear.

5

SPACES FOR GOOD CONVERSATIONS

There are always three sides to every story: your side, the other side, and the truth.

—Robert Evans

'If you are not with us, you must be against us,' President George W. Bush declared after 9/11, compelling people to declare whose side they were on. All the labour union leaders sat on one side of the big table at the meeting in Mumbai, and all the employers sat on the other side. This physical division made it easier to know which side they were on. We generally assume that everyone sitting on the same side of a legislative chamber or the same side of a table should have the same views. If someone we assumed was on our side supports what the other side is advocating, we are surprised. 'We thought you were on our side!' we say. Where we sit is expected to indicate where we stand in a debate. To make people's loyalties clear, it is customary in many legislative chambers to make people sit on opposing sides. People who change their minds and betray

WE WILL TELL YOU WHEN YOU CAN SPEAK!

our side must cross the floor and sit on the other side.

The Indian State has a federal structure. The states in the Indian Union have their own elected governments headed by their chief ministers. The Central government of the Union is also elected and is headed by a prime minister. For 63 years, until 2014, the prime minister chaired a Planning Commission for the whole country. The Planning Commission was replaced in 2015 by the NITI Aayog (the National Institution for the Transformation of India), which is chaired by the prime minister. The plans made by the Planning Commission (and now NITI Aayog) are developed under the guidance of the National Development Council (NDC), which is composed of the chief ministers of all states and the prime minister along with members of the Central cabinet, who are members of the Planning Commission. Thus, the NDC is the highest forum for planning the future of the country with the participation of all states.

Until 2014, meetings of the NDC were held in the central hall of the Vigyan Bhavan in New Delhi, the country's most prestigious meeting chamber. The central hall is a large auditorium that can seat a thousand people. Visiting heads of state and other dignitaries sit on a large and high stage above the front rows of the auditorium. In the meetings of the NDC, the PM and other Central government ministers would sit on stage. The chief ministers of the states would sit below them in the front rows of the auditorium. Behind them would be hundreds of officers of the Central and State governments and others invited to witness the meeting.

The meetings had an imperial aura to them. The PM and his colleagues on the stage were surrounded by masses of beautifully arranged flowers and silk banners. The people seated below looked up at them. The PM and others higher up on the stage made their speeches. Then, the 28 chief ministers were invited to speak by turn, for a few minutes each (with a buzzer to tell them when their time was over). Some four hours later, after their speeches, and when everyone was quite exhausted, the dignitaries on the stage would make some closing statements and the meeting would conclude. There were no questions asked. No answers given. No discussion. No deliberation.

Some chief ministers felt insulted. Dr J. Jayalalithaa, the mercurial and outspoken late chief minister of the large and rich southern state of Tamil Nadu, walked out of an NDC meeting, and told the media outside that she saw no reason to come to Delhi to be lectured on how to spend her own money! Narendra Modi, then chief minister of Gujarat, used his few minutes at the last meeting of the NDC in 2013, to make some critical comments about the format of the meeting. He said there was neither any discussion amongst the chief ministers at the meeting about issues that affected all of them, nor any deliberation with the PM and his colleagues. He insisted that the meeting was like a classroom in which the chief ministers were invited to be lectured to.

A few months after his election as the Prime Minister of India, Mr Modi convened a meeting of all the chief ministers to discuss the agenda for national plans. Bristling at the ignominy of the NDC meetings, he wanted the chief ministers to feel

SPACES FOR GOOD CONVERSATIONS

as equals in the meeting. He wanted them to be seated in a circle with the PM. His staff had a big problem. For security reasons, the meeting had to be held in a government building. They could not find a large room in any government building in New Delhi that could accommodate a large circle of people seated on the same level! All large rooms in these buildings were set up either like the auditorium in Vigyan Bhavan or like formal conference rooms with large, immovable tables. All rooms had been hard-wired for conventional, formal meetings.

The PM's solution was to lay out a large circle of chairs on the lawns of his house for a meeting with a different set-up to discuss a different way for planning the future of the country.

Changing the layout of the meeting was a good first step because it signalled an intention to change the pattern of the conversation. However, it could not change deeply embedded structures of thought and distribution of power. Therefore, the struggle between the centralization of power in India and the desirable devolution to State and City governments continues. Changes in institutional structures require deep changes in thought structures.

Nevertheless, since settings do have an effect on the quality of conversations, and since they are easier to change than institutional structures, one can make a beginning towards desirable changes with changed settings.

A meeting with a difference to discuss the future of India was held in Jaipur in February 2005. Its purpose was to provide an opportunity for leaders and emerging leaders from many walks of life in India to *pause and reflect together* on what they could do to enable desirable changes in the country. The meeting was unlike other meetings and seminars on the future of India. Three significant differences in its format facilitated deeper reflection on the future and present condition of the country amongst the hundred or so people who assembled together.

Firstly, the participants were very diverse. There was diversity of vocation—businessmen, politicians, bureaucrats, farmers, teachers, leaders of NGOs, students, journalists, homemakers, diplomats, and others. There was also diversity of age—from teenaged school students to retired cabinet secretaries in their seventies, and a healthy gender ratio—an equal number of men and women. The diversity of participants enabled many perspectives of the reality of India to be combined for all to understand the whole truth.

Second, the meeting was conducted in an open space in the gardens of the Rambagh Palace Hotel. The hotel created an informal, open amphitheatre for plenary sessions when all the participants were together. There were several groups of chairs spread out under the trees for smaller, parallel meetings. There were neither tables nor chairs in the amphitheatre. Layers of wooden platforms were set up in a horse-shoe format, with mattresses and cushions strewn on them. Participants could sit wherever they wanted.

Too many meetings are designed and conducted as meetings amongst positions and not meetings amongst people. People with higher positions must sit higher. People with the same positions on an issue must sit together. The settings of the meetings reinforce positions. They strengthen views of people as stereotypes. Moreover, they nestle people within their societal and ideological boxes from which they are expected to speak.

When Ms Vasundhara Raje, the Chief Minister of Rajasthan, came to the opening session of the meeting, she saw the diverse people—young and old, rich and poor (wealthy women in silk saris and farmers in white cotton dhotis), seniors and juniors—seated together on the mattresses. The organizers had placed a chair for her in the front. But she walked past it, climbed onto a platform, and settled down on a mattress amongst the people.

The third difference between the Jaipur meeting and conventional meetings was in the design of the meeting. It was designed as a dialogue amongst participants, rather than as a series of monologues that many meetings tend to be. There was no assigned time for speeches, nor any designated speakers, except for the brief introductions in the opening session about the purpose of the meeting and principles for its successful conduct.

Three principles were laid down for the meeting:

- The difficult and seemingly intractable problems in India, whether poor governance or endemic corruption, require collaboration amongst people from many walks of life. They cannot be solved by government, business, or civic society alone. Therefore, pointing fingers at others for failing to solve the problems does not help much. In fact, we have

to identify and accept our own responsibilities, because 'if we are not part of the problem, we cannot be part of the solution.'
- In the meeting, all people will be equals and will get equal opportunities to express themselves and be heard, whether they are a young student or a senior bureaucrat, because we can all learn from the benefit of insights from other perspectives.
- The primary orientation of every participant in the meeting must be to *listen* and to *learn*, and not try yet again to convince (with arguments that are stuck in our heads and that we repeat in multiple forums).

No doubt, the open setting made a big difference to the quality of the meeting. The principles for the conduct of the meeting, which the participants asked me, as their facilitator, to apply firmly, made an even bigger difference. Everyone got an equal opportunity to speak, whether a student, homemaker, farmer or a chief minister. Just as in a computer, in which the configuration of the hardware and the design of the software give the computer its capability to convert data to decisions, the design of the setting and the process enables a meeting to combine ideas of diverse people into agreements.

In the concluding plenary session in the amphitheatre, one of the participants, Ms Lata Vaidyanathan, the principal of a Delhi school, requested permission to read a poem she had composed to express her feelings about the meeting. She stepped into the open space before the participants and recited this:

SPACES FOR GOOD CONVERSATIONS

I wandered and wondered
Like a lonely bird in the sky
With none but the clouds to encounter
When a gentle tapping breeze
Turned me around

I saw a flock of birds come
Who seemed to say
If we move together
The clouds will help us to sail
For there are rainbows in the yonder
For all of us to hail

We have sighted our target
And need to decide that
If we move together
Nothing is hard to get

Let each one be special
But knit our strengths around
For we want a country
That's first on the count.

The design of the physical settings of meetings—the hardware—can have a tremendous impact on the quality of meetings. Conveners of meetings must pay more attention to the settings to achieve their desired outcomes. In addition to the hardware, the software of meetings—processes for dialogue and deliberation—enable deeper listening thereby improving outcomes of conversations and meetings.

6

Lenses and Stereotypes

Most people are other people. Their thoughts are someone else's opinions, their lives a mimicry, their passions a quotation.

—Oscar Wilde

Sometimes we must dunk our heads beneath 'the water-line' to see things that we cannot see when we keep our heads above water. We need to undertake the difficult task of looking inside our own minds to see what is going on unconsciously in the backs of our own heads. It is important to understand some of the structures that shape our thinking about others and the world. In our explorations beneath the water-line, we will be guided by the studies of patterns of thought and perceptions in human minds undertaken by psychologists and sociologists.

Seeing beneath the water-line is not easy, and this reliance on the research of academics may feel a little hard to navigate. However, it will give us insight into what goes on in the backs of our minds.

PUTTING PEOPLE INTO BOXES

Who I am will determine what I buy, according to marketers. Market planners divide people into market segments depending on who they are: their level of income, level of education, age, sex, race, where they live, etc. They are constantly searching for better definitions of market segments into which they can divide people and looking for better ways to box us into categories.

Who I am will also determine who I will vote for, according to political pollsters. Pollsters too divide us into segments depending on our race, sex, education, age, occupation, etc. The accuracy of pollsters' predictions depends on how precisely they can categorize us and how accurately they can determine which way we will vote depending on who we are. When their predictions go wrong (as they often do), they have to go back to the drawing board to identify the flaws in their segmentation of voters and predictions of ways in which each segment would vote.

Marketers and pollsters know that who we are will determine what we care about and the choices we will make. So they categorize us and box us. Those put in the same box are all the same from their perspective.

As we go about our own lives, we also categorize the people we encounter. We also put them into boxes and see them as stereotypes. We instinctively respond to them and judge them according to the stereotype we see them as, i.e., the mental box we put them into. By boxing and stereotyping the people we encounter, the computers in our minds are programmed to give us default reactions towards them.

If a white person encounters a young black man in a narrow alley, his/her instinct will be to exercise caution because the latter could be dangerous. However, the default reaction could be faulty. The young black man may be a school teacher in a mixed community school, well-loved by all his students and respected by their parents. He would be most likely to assist the white person, if she needed help, rather than harm her.

Stereotyping others makes our reactions towards them much quicker because we don't have to examine each person individually to understand who the real person is behind the label our mind puts on him. Like marketers and pollsters, we need to categorize people to come to conclusions efficiently. And we can be very wrong too.

How we see the world around us and how we react to others also depends on who we are. A black man would react differently than a white woman would if he sees another black man in the alley. A Muslim would react differently on seeing a woman in a burqa than someone from another religion. One would be reassured to be in the midst of his own people amongst whom it is the custom for women not to expose their faces in modesty. The other may apprehend a threat behind the covers.

Our personal histories provide us with lenses through which we see the world and with which we evaluate others. Our lenses colour what we see, and also filter out some things that we do not see even if they are right before our eyes. For example, an economist and a sociologist surveying a bazaar will notice different things. The economist will note the buzz of transactions and circulation of money, and the haggling over prices. The sociologist may pay more attention to differences between what men and women do in the market, and also the ways in which owners of shops and their employees relate to each other. To the economist, the bazaar is principally a buzzing market for things, while to the sociologist, it is a buzzing community place for encounters amongst diverse people. The economist and the sociologist may be of the same race, religion and age too. Nevertheless, the sociologist may seem blind to inefficiencies in the market, whereas the economist may be equally blind to indignities in the relationships between people.

DIFFERENT LENSES

There are many differences amongst us that make us see the world differently. I will explain such differences with three examples—

1. Differences on account of gender: Gender lenses
2. Differences on account of race, culture and geography: Cultural lenses
3. Differences on account of education: Epistemic lenses

GENDER LENSES

'You think so much like a man. You don't get my point of view at all,' my wife complains sometimes. And I often fret that she is so impractical and so emotional—like most women.

LENSES AND STEREOTYPES

'Why can't a woman be more like a man?' Prof. Henry Higgins wonders in the American musical *My Fair Lady*: 'Why do they do everything their mothers do? Why don't they grow up—well, like their father instead?'

The highest ranked work of non-fiction of the 1990s, according to CNN, was the book by American author and relationship counsellor John Gray—*Men are from Mars, Women are from Venus*.[11] It spent 121 weeks on the bestseller list and sold more than 50 million copies all over the world. Most common relationship problems between men and women, Gray explains, are because they see the world very differently. He exemplifies this with the metaphor that men and women are from separate planets—men from Mars and women from Venus, and though they may live together on Earth, each sex is acclimatized to its own planet's societies and customs.

Thank goodness men and women are different! I imagine the world would be a boring place—for both men and women—if there were no biological as well as psychological differences between them. However, value judgements about who is superior and who is inferior make relationships amongst them inequitable. (Henry Higgins clearly thinks women are inferior. They should not grow up like their mothers and they should become more like men.)

Differences amongst persons make it difficult for them to see 'eye to eye'. John Gray explains how men and women

---

[11] Gray, John, *Men Are from Mars, Women Are from Venus*, HarperCollins, 1992.

have different perspectives. Along with a different perspective, a feeling of superiority—of being on a higher level than the other—makes it even more difficult to see 'eye to eye'. Over thousands of years of human history, men have been accustomed to feeling superior to women and to dominating women within their families and their societies.

The internationally acclaimed scholar Riane Eisler has recorded the origins of misogyny going back thousands of years. Excavations at many sites around the Middle East have revealed pictures and statuettes that illuminate cultures in Neolithic times, some 8,000 to 10,000 years ago. In these cultures, women were highly respected as the producers of life. Goddesses were worshiped more than gods. In pictures on pots and friezes, women are seen sitting alongside and, sometimes, even above men in community meetings. Eisler's scholarly book *The Chalice and the Blade* sold over half a million copies within a few years.[12] It was also a primary source for *The Da Vinci Code*, Dan Brown's book which sold in millions.

Eisler records how men began to assert themselves in societies and rose to dominate them thousands of years ago, and how since then they have systematically subjugated women. God became a powerful and wrathful man in Middle Eastern myths and religions thousands of years ago—the God of the Old Testament of the Bible, whereas the earlier Goddess was a nurturing woman. Jesus appeared as a reformer of an

---

[12]Eisler, Riane Tennenhaus, *The Chalice and the Blade: Our History, Our Future*, HarperCollins, 1987.

unjust society. He preached a different message in the New Testament—of love, compassion, forgiveness and 'turning the other cheek'. He stood up for the weak and the oppressed against the power of autocratic rulers and priests, all of whom were males in his time. Eisler's speculation, based on historical records, that Jesus was taking 'affirmative action' two thousand years before it was found necessary in the twentieth century society to correct millennia of injustice to women, inspired Dan Brown's *The Da Vinci Code*. Dan Brown's page-turning story claims that Jesus had actually chosen a woman as his successor and since then a secret organization in the Church has ruthlessly squashed any remaining evidence of Jesus's intent.

The lenses through which we see and judge others are built into our psyches by myths and stories. We are told these myths and stories by our parents and teachers, by the priests in our temples and churches, and by scholars who record the histories of our civilizations. Myths that some people are inherently superior are pervasive in our communities and our minds. They shape our lenses and make it hard for us to see others at the same level and to see them eye to eye. With our differences in perception and with our perceptions of differences amongst us, we are unable to understand who the other person actually is behind the stereotype in our mind.

CULTURAL LENSES

People with black skin and people with white skin are visibly different. There is little they can do to change the colour of their skins, since it is all about genetics. They are born with it. Another aspect that plays an important role in this is where they come from—the geography. There they grow up in societies with different histories and different cultures. Their communities share different myths and tell different stories. Hence, it is not surprising that there are many differences in the lenses everyone wears and their ways of seeing the world.

However, geography does not tell the whole story of differences. White and black people have lived together for centuries in the US. Yet, they are still not considered equal. The belief in the superiority of white people persists, even though the United States Declaration of Independence says, 'We hold these truths to be self-evident, that all men are created equal...' Inequality is evident in many insensitive encounters between white and black people. Young black men are far more likely to be viewed as sources of trouble by white policemen, regardless of the facts.

A more egregious example is the caste system in India, which has persisted for centuries. Many upper caste persons continue to believe that it is their birthright to look down upon lower castes. Declarations of equality in the Indian Constitution cannot easily change habits of thought and behaviour embedded in the minds of Indian citizens.

We often think of entire classes of people as inferior. Often I have heard well-to-do and 'well-educated' women in a social gathering in a luxurious apartment talk about their domestic help. 'You cannot trust *these* people', someone says. '*They* are like that.' 'What can one do,' another says, '*we* have to tolerate them.' '*They* smell different too,' says a perfumed and bejewelled matron. These women are not talking about lower caste people specifically. They are 'people like us' talking about 'people who are not like us'. Listening to these prejudices, I often recall white-skinned, blue-eyed Joe Curry listening intently to our dark-skinned, barefooted cook Augustin beside our dining table in Pune, forty years ago. They connected as two human beings, who for a few deep moments became people like each other, despite their many differences.

Contrary to the 'self-evident' truth that all men are created equal, human history is replete with oppression of some people by others justified with a belief in their own superiority—men over women (it is noteworthy that the US Constitution adopted in 1789 did not consider women equal to men), whites over blacks, as mentioned before, and Western nations over the nations they colonized.

For over three centuries, white merchants, soldiers and priests from European countries, and their extensions in North America, Australia and South Africa, spread the power of white men, along with a belief in the superiority of Western civilization, around the world. They looked down on all coloured people—black, brown and yellow people. European powers self-justified their colonization of other countries as bearing the 'white man's burden' of civilizing inferior natives.

The complete victory of the Japanese military over Russia in the early years of the twentieth century surprised Western nations. It was the first big blow to the invincibility of white men. After Japan's defeat in the Second World War with the horrifying devastation of Hiroshima and Nagasaki (the first and only time nuclear bombs have been deliberately used on a civilian population to terrorize its people), Japan rose up again. Its industries developed surprisingly fast after the War, and conquered the world. Japanese producers of automobiles, electronics, metals, machinery and home appliances seemed invincible with their high quality and low costs.

China's breaking out of its subservience to the West (and Japan) took longer. China's history was churned after the Second World War by its internal revolutions. Since then, with its remarkable economic progress, it has become the second largest economy in the world, and has emerged as the other pole of global power contending with the US, a position the Soviet Union had until it collapsed.

After the Second World War, India finally broke out of the grip of its colonial rulers, following a long, non-violent fight for its freedom led by Mahatma Gandhi. It became a leading light for anti-colonial movements around the world. In 1934, when the Jewish nationalist Ben Gurion tried to convince the Palestinian nationalist Musa Alami that Zionism would be a 'blessing to the Arabs of Palestine', bringing progress and development, Alami replied bluntly, 'I would prefer that the country remain impoverished and barren for another hundred years, until we ourselves are able to develop it on our own.'[13] Israel has now advanced much farther than Palestine in

---

[13] Teveth, Shabtai, *Ben-Gurion and the Palestinian Arabs: From Peace to War*, Oxford University Press, 1985, p 132.

LENSES AND STEREOTYPES

material terms. The Palestinians continue to struggle for their independence and respect.

Asians have become accustomed to seeing themselves through Western eyes: to judge how much they have progressed by how far behind they are from the West. It was also usual for them to be talked down to by Westerners and to value the advice of Western experts as superior to their own experts. The economic and political rise of Japan, China, India and other Asian countries over the past 25 years, along with a slowing down of growth in the West, has begun to shift the centre of gravity of world affairs from the West to Asia. Western superiority has diminished. Now Asians are beginning to once again think that their own way of seeing the world may not be inferior after all.

Indeed, even in the West, as signs of Asian success emerged, there has been a growing curiosity, and even admiration, for Asian ways. When Japanese companies began to conquer markets around the world, Western business scholars pointed out that Japanese people worked very well in teams, whereas Americans were individualists. According to them, Japanese people do not like to stand out from their peers. 'Any nail that stands out is hammered down,' is the Japanese way, they said.

The much mysterious China has always fascinated the West. With China's remarkable economic resurgence, people have become even more curious about the seemingly inscrutable Chinese mind. When India emerged, without violence, as a free and democratic nation, an interest in Indian traditions of spirituality, yoga and religion increased in the West.

Do Asians think differently than Westerners? Do they see the world through different lenses? Psychologist Richard E. Nisbett reports the conclusions of tests conducted by him and other psychologists. He explains their findings in his book *The Geography of Thought: How Asians and Westerners Think Differently…and Why*.[14]

The studies indicate that to Asians the world is 'a complex place understandable in terms of the whole rather than in terms of the parts', and 'subject to more collective than personal control'. Whereas to the Westerner, the world is 'a relatively simple place, composed of discrete objects that can be understood without undue attention to context' and is 'highly subject to personal control'.

Consistent with these differences in worldviews, surveys also show that Asians feel themselves to be less in control than their Western counterparts. Rather than attempting to control situations, they are likely to adjust to them. Other evidence, says Nesbitt, also suggests that, 'Feeling in control is not as important for Asians as it is for Westerners. And whereas Westerners seem to believe it's crucial for them to have direct, personal control, Asians seem to believe outcomes will be better for them if they are simply in the same boat with others.'

Confirmation of this observation that Asians accept suffering when they are in the same boat came when the Indian Government suddenly withdrew over 80 per cent

---

[14] Nisbett, Richard E., *The Geography of Thought: How Asians and Westerners Think Differently…and Why*, Free Press, 2003.

of the currency from the economy in November 2016. The government's stated aim at the outset was to hurt the rich and corrupt people, who had accumulated a lot of wealth. However, poor people with no bank accounts, and those who are paid in cash, and those whose small enterprises operate only in cash, suffered the most. They could not buy food and daily necessities. They lost their jobs. Their enterprises closed. Millions stood in long queues at banks, some for hours, waiting to exchange the few old notes they had, which had been declared illegal, with the new ones that were scarce because the government's mints were unable to print enough. Yet, to the surprise of economists who expected a mass uprising, there was little trouble. Along with others, people endured their pain, reassured that they were all in the same boat.

Development psychologist Joan Miller compared Hindu East Indians and Americans. She asked her middle-aged, middle-class participants to 'describe the behaviour of an acquaintance that they considered a wrong thing to have done and behaviour on the part of an acquaintance they considered good for someone else'. She then asked the participants to explain why the people behaved the way they did. American participants explained the behaviour in terms of personality traits of the actor, such as 'X is considerate and friendly'. Indians tended to explain behaviour in terms of contextual factors, such as 'the old woman needed help and there was no one else around to help her'. Indians, Miller reports, gave twice as many contextual explanations as Americans did.[15]

These psychologists' studies suggest that Asians pay attention to the context more than their American counterparts. A generalization from these studies is that Asians view the world through wide-angle lenses whereas Westerners have tunnel vision.

However, we must be cautious. Just as, generally speaking, 'women are from Venus and men from Mars' and have different worldviews, the contrasts between the ways Westerners and Asians see the world, noted by Nisbett, Miller, and other psychologists, are generalizations. There are billions of Asians, and almost a billion Westerners. All Westerners are not the same and neither are all Asians. Amongst the billions of Asians, there are likely to be many millions of Asians who think more like Westerners than like other Asians. Similarly, amongst Westerners, there would be millions who think more like Asians.

Therein lies the problem with stereotypes—of Westerners and Asians, Muslims and non-Muslims, Jew and Gentiles. Their different histories, cultures and beliefs give them different lenses through which they see the world. They also have different markers of their identity that distinguishes them from each other: such as the languages they speak, the ways they dress, and the food they prefer. By such markers, one may quickly conclude who the person is. But one could

---

[15]Miller, Joan, 'Culture and Development of Everyday Social Explanation', *Journal of Personality and Social Psychology*, Vol. 46, 1984.

very well be wrong because beneath these visible markers lies a great diversity.

A divide that is dangerously deepening in the world is between Muslims and the rest. There are 1.6 billion Muslims in the world. There is great diversity amongst them, just as there is amongst the 2.6 billion Christians and the 1 billion Hindus. There are white Muslims, black Muslims and brown Muslims, just as there are white, black and brown Christians. Christians speak many different languages, just as Muslims do. Christians follow different versions of their religion, as do Muslims. Conflicts amongst Christians can be bloody, as they can be amongst Muslims too. The Middle East is aflame with clashes amongst Muslims. Europe was riven with bloody wars in the Middle Ages between Catholic and Protestant Christians. Regardless of the diversity amongst Muslims, there is a dangerous trend now to paint all Muslims the same colour with one big, broad brush.

Samuel Huntington's hypothesis in his book *The Clash of Civilizations and the Remaking of World Order* said that the post-Cold War world would be marked by civilizational conflict between human beings divided along cultural lines—Western, Islamic, Hindu and so on.[16] He saw the West as one cultural block, which included Christian and Jewish cultures, though there are religious and cultural differences amongst them. He warned that a clash was immanent between the West and

---

[16] Huntington, Samuel P., *The Clash of Civilizations and the Remaking of World Order*, Simon & Schuster, 1992.

Islam. Ominously, Donald Trump, in his inaugural address as 45th President of the US, has called on the 'civilized world' to unite against radical Islamic terrorism.

EPISTEMIC LENSES

As we continue our exploration underwater of the lenses we wear and the stereotypes of others in the backs of our minds, there are some parts of the discussion that may appear to be academic. Indeed, they are about academics!

Three decades before Samuel Huntington wrote *The Clash of Civilizations*, British scientist and novelist C.P. Snow wrote *The Two Cultures and the Scientific Revolution*. In 2008, the Times Literary Supplement included *The Two Cultures and the Scientific Revolution* in its list of the 100 books that most influenced Western public discourse since the Second World War. Snow's thesis was that the intellectual life of the whole of Western society was split into two cultures—namely the sciences and the humanities—and that this was a major hindrance to solving the world's problems.

Snow's position can be summed up by an often-repeated part of his essay:

> A good many times I have been present at gatherings of people who, by the standards of the traditional culture, are thought highly educated and who have with considerable gusto been expressing their incredulity at the illiteracy of scientists. Once or twice I have been provoked and have

asked the company how many of them could describe the Second Law of Thermodynamics. The response was cold; it was also negative. Yet I was asking something which is the scientific equivalent of: *Have you read a work of Shakespeare's?* I now believe that if I had asked an even simpler question—such as, What do you mean by mass, or acceleration, which is the scientific equivalent of saying, *Can you read?*—not more than one in ten of the highly educated would have felt that I was speaking the same language. So the great edifice of modern physics goes up, and the majority of the cleverest people in the western world have about as much insight into it as their Neolithic ancestors would have had.[17]

Epistemology is the branch of philosophy that investigates methods of acquiring knowledge. It examines how we know what we know, and how we know that it is the truth. Snow pointed out the two different ways in which Western people were being 'educated'. One set made sense of the world through the art and stories of playwrights, poets and philosophers. The other set made sense of the world through the experiments and theories of scientists. The different types of education give these persons, who are racially and culturally the same, different 'epistemic' lenses through which they see the world. And, just like Rudyard Kipling said 'the West is West and the East is East and never the twain shall meet', Snow said these two sets

---

[17] Snow, C.P., The Rede Lecture delivered on 7 May 1959 at the University of Cambridge.

WHERE IS THE ELEPHANT?

of people could not see eye to eye.

The Planning Commission of India was charged with making plans for 'inclusive, sustainable, and faster growth' of the Indian economy. The breadth of the Commission's charter required many perspectives to be combined. Therefore, it brought together eight members with diverse backgrounds. Amongst us was Dr Krishnaswamy Kasturirangan, an eminent scientist and former chairman of the very successful Indian Space Research Organization (ISRO), and Dr Syeda Hameed, a respected social activist and novelist with doctoral degrees in social sciences from the US and Canada, and the only woman amongst us. The Planning Commission was dominated by economists: there were four, with different specializations and ideologies. The other members were a retired bureaucrat and myself. I was the only person who had worked as a manager in the private sector; my formal education is as a physicist.

We would meet twice a month to consider various issues, ranging from the state of education, the security of women in the country, to the quantum of financial resources required to meet economic growth targets. With the members seeing issues through their diverse lenses, the meetings would throw a broad light on the country's multi-faceted challenges. Often though, with the 'clash of cultures' Snow had noted, there would be more heat and less light in the meetings. The sole woman amongst us would say the economists' numbers were not making any sense. She would demand they explain themselves in 'simple English'.

Syeda travelled the country extensively, especially to the rural, tribal and so-called 'backward' areas where the poorest people in the country lived. She listened to the people who were not yet uplifted by the rising tide of global growth, and whose lives had not been improved much by successive Five Year Plans drawn up by the Planning Commission. She said she could not see the reality of their lives in the cold numbers and mathematical equations the economists presented. Often it was left to me, Dr Kasturirangan or B.K. Chaturvedi, the three 'non-economist' members of the Planning Commission, to be the bridge between the two epistemic cultures within the Planning Commission, and to calm down the arguments which could become quite heated.

Syeda urged the Deputy Chairman of the Planning Commission, Dr Montek Singh Ahluwalia, to convene an 'offsite' meeting of the members in which we could talk heart-to-heart in plain English. Montek asked me to design and facilitate the meeting. The quality of conversation in this meeting was very different to the discussions in the Planning Commission's formal meetings. We talked about our aspirations for the impact we wanted our work to have on the lives of people in India. We became quite candid about the gaps between our aspirations and reality. There was a resolve to change the ways we made plans, and to engage more widely with civil society organizations and other stakeholders. An outcome of the meeting was the development of a systematic process for involving almost a thousand organizations to develop the approach for the next Five Year Plan, which I have described earlier in the book.

In his essay, Snow showed his preference for the scientific

way rather than the ways of the humanities to improve the world. Development of 'scientific' minds that sought 'rational' and 'objective' explanations of reality was a principal driver of the Enlightenment that emerged in Europe in the seventeenth century. Scientific discoveries were translated into machines, new methods of transportation and communication, and powerful weapons. Another strong driver of the Enlightenment ideas was belief in the rights of individual humans and in their agency to shape their lives. These two strands flowed into the evolution of economics as a social science, with its core tenet of human beings as rational, self-interested actors.

The science-driven Enlightenment emanating from Western Europe in the seventeenth century enabled the West to conquer the rest of the world. New weapons and new methods of transportation and communication, as well as new kinds of entrepreneurial organizations, were more effective than the resources others had. The military and economic domination of the West (which was almost entirely white and Christian) over the rest, proved that its ways were superior and that the ways of blacks, browns, Asians, Africans, Muslims and Hindus were inferior.

The years from 2009–14 were difficult for the world economy after the global financial crisis. Global problems and several internal difficulties had begun to affect India's economic growth. Many large projects were mired in controversies, so both investors and banks were reluctant to risk more money; and a nation wide anti-corruption movement was putting the administration into a mode of caution and pause. Combinations of external and internal uncertainties made it very difficult for the economists of the Planning Commission to forecast the future and set goals for the Indian economy.

Very few economists managed to predict the global economic recession. Many forces interact dynamically to change economic conditions. Globalization has connected the economies of many countries together. What happens in one country will quickly affect the others. The collapse of Lehman Brothers in the US caused a global financial meltdown. The Internet, 24×7 news channels, and social media can change 'moods' and 'sentiments' that can affect stock markets and create panic in foreign exchange markets as well.

Economists require models of the salient forces that shape an economy. They must have mathematical equations into which they can put values of these forces, which they can run on computers to compute the state of the economy in future. The models of the Indian economy which India's economic planners had been using did not fit the economy any more. The shape of the economy had changed with the loosening of internal controls and the increasing openness of the Indian economy to the world since the 1990s. A project was undertaken by the Planning Commission in 2009 to develop an up-to-date model of the Indian economy. Several economic research organizations in India, each of whom had a model of the economy, were invited to share their models, with the expectation that a combination of them could provide a more reliable guide to India's policymakers and economic forecasters.

Some economists admit they suffer from physics envy.

They aspire to model complex socio-economic phenomena in the way physicists model natural phenomena. Physicists have methods to make good models of complex systems. Using mathematical equations derived from their models, they can make remarkably accurate predictions. Thus, they are able to control the trajectories of rockets and the flight paths of satellites to land them on distant planets. Dr Montek Singh Ahluwalia invited the two physicists in the Planning Commission—Dr Kasturirangan and me—to a meeting in which the economic research organizations presented their models and debated their features amongst themselves. He was curious to know if we could help in improving the structure of the models.

Dr Kasturirangan and I sat close to each other like friends in a strange forest, in a room full of economists with their equations and numbers flashing across projection screens. We wondered what the models were trying to represent. We could not see the forest or the trees. Afterwards, Montek asked me for our impressions. I said I could do no better than reproduce the record of a meeting called by Kenneth Arrow and Brian Arthur, Nobel laureates in economics in 1987.

Arrow and Arthur arranged a meeting of economists with physicists, including Nobel laureates Murray Gell-Mann and Phil Anderson, to understand what economists may learn from physicists about the formulation of theories and models.

M. Mitchel Waldorp gives an account of the meeting in his book *Complexity: The Emerging Science at the Edge of Order and Chaos*—

And indeed, as the axioms and theorems and proofs marched across the overhead projector screen, the physicists could only be awestruck at their counterparts' mathematical prowess—awestruck and appalled. They had the same objection that Arthur and many other economists had been voicing from within the field for years. 'They were almost too good,' says one young physicist, who remembers shaking his head in disbelief. 'It seemed as though they were dazzling themselves with fancy mathematics, until they really couldn't see the forest for the trees. So much time was being spent on trying to absorb the mathematics that I thought they weren't often looking at what the models were for, and what they did, and whether the underlying assumptions were any good. In a lot of cases, what was required was just some common sense.'[18]

I told Montek that in all fairness, economists must be dealing with a more complex world than physicists. Economics is a social science, which must understand and then model the behaviour of human beings. Human beings have feelings and passions. Fundamental particles, atoms and molecules—the constituents of the systems that physicists model and represent in their equations—have no such qualities. They can be represented as pure quantities. Human beings are much harder to quantify. Therefore, the predictions from mathematical models of

---

[18] Waldrop, M. Mitchell, *Complexity: The Emerging Science at the Edge of Order and Chaos*, Penguin, 1994.

economies are bound to go wrong when human fears and aspirations, which cannot be accurately quantified, change the condition of the system. What economists need is a method to explain a system with all the forces in it including those that cannot be quantified.

TOWARDS A NEW INTEGRATIVE ENLIGHTENMENT

St Andrews in Scotland is world-renowned for two things. It was a fountainhead for the European Enlightenment. It is the third oldest university in the English-speaking world. Amongst those who wrote and taught in St Andrews was Adam Smith, often regarded as the father of economics, to whom a fundamental tenet of economics is attributed, viz. that human beings are rational, self-interested actors.

St Andrews is also known worldwide as the home of golf. On 14 May 1754, 22 noblemen and gentlemen of Fife formed themselves into 'The Society of St Andrews Golfers'. In 1834, King William IV became the society's patron, conferring on it the title of 'Royal and Ancient Golf Club of St Andrews', which, as any serious golfer knows, has been of central importance in the evolution of the game worldwide.

Unlike the 22 noblemen who had gathered there in May 1754, not one of the 24 people who had assembled at the club in April 2001 (including myself) had any intention to play golf, despite being housed on the very edge of one of the world's most hallowed golf courses. Around them were pictures and mementos of the legends that had played at that course over the past 150 years: Bobby Jones, Arnold Palmer and Jack Nicklaus from the twentieth century, and others, too, from the nineteenth century. The Old Course was at their feet, and the other courses of St Andrews lay just beyond.

These 24 people, who came from the UK, US, Europe, South Africa and India, were economists, businessmen, technologists, scientists, philosophers and artists. They had been invited by the Scottish Council Foundation and British Petroleum for an unusual purpose: to change the world. Naturally, they had no time for golf!

What was the compulsion for the meeting? Here is what the sponsors said:

> Perhaps every generation has the sense that it is uniquely challenged: by the speed of change, the direction of change, the scale of change. What Hobsbawm called 'the short twentieth century' certainly brought massive transformation on a global scale.
>
> Yet there is mounting evidence to suggest that we are today living through changes that are faster, bigger and more fundamental than ever before in human history. Our knowledge about the world is unprecedented, as is the level of communication across the globe, the pace of development of new technologies and many other phenomena. In consequence, almost everywhere we look what used to be the stuff of dreams can now be contemplated in terms of practical reality. Whether or not we decide to do it, we know how to clone a human

being, how to prolong human life, how to feed the world, how to facilitate the operation of a global consciousness. What previously might have been erudite questions for philosophers have now become practical choices for individuals and societies. We are living in a world in which almost anything seems possible, yet in which the forces of fragmentation and alienation seem at least as strong as those of integration and mindfulness: we seem short of the wisdom to choose which possibilities to explore and which to deny.[19]

These 24 people were gathered together under the banner of the International Futures Forum. Their brief was to develop an agenda for learning and action over the next two years, which would include many others in many parts of the world, to find a solution to a universal problem. A problem caused by the clash of forces of fragmentation and alienation with forces of integration and mindfulness.

The enormity of the undertaking, and the anxiety about our ability to live up to what was expected of us by our sponsors, was very humbling. We wondered where to begin. It was absolutely unlike a round of golf, in which there is a designated spot to tee off from and a direction to shoot, with a very definite objective: a precise little hole to shoot for.

As we were flapping in the wind, not knowing where to

---

[19]From the letter of invitation by the Scottish Council Foundation to participants of the first meeting of the International Futures Forum in St Andrews, Scotland, April 2001.

start and where to get to, our facilitator reminded us of a lesson he had learned as a Boy Scout. Using the apt analogy of putting up a tent in the wind, he suggested that we get our hands onto whatever part of the canvas we could get hold of, and start putting some stakes in the ground. We could then adjust the shape of the tent as we went along. He also warned us that we would fail if we tried to put up one stake at a time. The three or more stakes of the tent must come up together to support each other so that they can stand. Making his point clearer, he used the analogy of a house of cards—only when all the cards come together will the house stand.

Each of us was determinedly holding on to a stake: our way of making sense of the world. We would have to cooperate with each other, listen to each other, and adjust our thinking as we went along, he said. Only then would the tent—our house of knowledge—stand.

An epistemic problem with the scientific way is its drive to understand the properties of individual components of a system more thoroughly in the belief that the mystery of the whole can be explained from the properties of its parts. Since the Enlightenment, the domains of sciences have expanded. At the same time, sciences have been breaking down into narrower specializations, each knowing more and more about less and less. Now the parts must be put together to know the whole. The disciplines must talk and listen to each other to understand the whole. But this is not easy. The disciplines have their own lenses and their own jargons. They cannot understand each other. Nor do they seem to like each other!

LENSES AND STEREOTYPES

A vital difference amongst people is in how they look at 'systems'. In one view, the properties of the individual *components* of a system are the primary drivers of a systems' performance. In the other view, *relationships* between the components of a system are the primary drivers of its quality. Psychologists inquiring into the differences between Western and Asian lenses have noted that Westerners tend to focus on the actions of individuals, whereas Asians are more likely to take a wide-angle view and look at the context for individual actions. Eisler says that women, more often than men, tend to think of relationships and sense systems as a whole. The quality of our knowledge of the whole is deteriorating while we 'scientifically' pursue knowledge more sharply within compartments, about slices of reality and its infinitesimal particles.

Women are generally different to men, psychologists tell us. Very broadly, black people would be culturally different to whites because they are from different continents with different histories. More particularly, someone brought up in the US will have different experiences to someone brought up in Vietnam. Physicists and poets are likely to see the truth through different eyes. However, boxing people into categories does not help us to know who they are.

Consider this: one person is a female, black, Muslim physicist whose family has lived for generations in the US. The other is a male, white, Christian poet who was born and raised in India. Into which boxes shall we put them? Should we stereotype one as a black woman like all the other black women, and the other as a white male like all the other white males? Will one always think like a Westerner and the other as an Asian, always? The truth is that each is a unique combination of many differences. Therefore, we must pause to consider the *real* person behind the stereotypes of her or him in our minds.

We must learn to listen to people who are not like us to know who they are, and to know what they care about most deeply, which often turns out to be what we, as human beings, care about too. We are different. And, for many reasons, culturally as well as in the epistemic context, we think differently. None of us can see the whole truth by ourselves. As the wise facilitator in St Andrews had cautioned the people assembled there, we must listen to others to discover the whole truth together.

We have broken down knowledge, and we are also breaking down into narrower societies, behind walls, to protect ourselves from people who are not like us. We have to shake off such habits. We have to cross the walls to meet others. We need a new integrative Enlightenment to bring closer together people with different histories and diverse worldviews.

7

Building and Crossing Bridges

We have been all the way to the moon and back,
But have trouble crossing the street to meet the new neighbour.

—His Holiness the Dalai Lama, 'The Paradox of Our Age'

We know now why it is difficult to listen to others, especially those we consider 'people not like us'. Our different lenses, through which we make sense of the world around us, each in our own ways, make it hard for us to understand each other and to converge on the same view of the world. Therefore, conversations amongst us are very often contentious, and we are unable to come to agreements.

Our inability to agree with others, who we may not 'like' on social media and in real life too, is creating many problems for all of us. Hence, we must find ways to bridge the differences amongst us and work together for improving the world for everyone. Our conversations with others are bridges between us. The quality of these conversations determines the strength of the bridge we build. It is, therefore, imperative that we

WHOSE SIDE IS GOD ON?

understand the construction of conversations that can build strong bridges between diverse people.

In 1845, American philosopher Henry David Thoreau built himself a simple cabin beside Walden Pond in Massachusetts, so that he could retreat from the chatter of society into solitude and gather his own thoughts. He had only three chairs in his cabin. One, he said, was for solitude; two and three were for conversation and society respectively. On one, he could sit to read and write, and watch the trees turn golden in the autumn, the geese settle on the pond as winter approached, the flurry of snow outside, and the trees turn green again in the spring. Sitting on that chair, he could also listen to his own thoughts detached from others, while the seasons changed, undisturbed by him, outside.

Settings affect our thoughts. I am more likely to find mindspace to reflect on the content of this book while sitting in a quiet corner of a garden with my phone switched off than in a stadium with thousands of cheering sports fans. Whether participants in a meeting will be comfortable exposing their own feelings and exploring others' feelings would also depend on the setting of the conversation and how it is conducted. Two persons seated on two chairs, looking each other in the eye, with the snow gently falling outside the window, are in a space in which they can listen to each other and to their own thoughts too. They are unlikely to do this during a discussion in a TV studio, with others around them, in the glare of spotlights, and with thousands of viewers watching.

We cannot see the lenses in our own eyes through our own

eyes. We can see them reflected in another's eyes—if we look calmly and deeply into it. We cannot hear our own mind with our own mind. Similarly, we cannot easily see or hear what is going on in the back of our minds. Whereas others can reflect back to us—what they see and hear—if we are willing to listen to them. Only through each other's eyes and minds can we discover who 'we' are.

RICHNESS AND REACH OF CONVERSATIONS

I would now like to introduce a conceptual map of conversations, which has two axes. Along the north-south, or vertical axis, I plot the 'richness' of conversations. Up on top are shallow conversations in which participants merely share data about their surroundings. Deep down are dialogues in which minds and hearts are connected.

Conversations are shallow when merely data is exchanged. 'It is raining outside.' 'India beat England in the cricket test match yesterday.' They go deeper when opinions are shared. 'I think it rains too much in England.' 'I think the English team is playing very poorly.' Our opinions begin to reveal our feelings. Conversations go even deeper when we begin to explain why we feel the way we do. 'I become very miserable when it rains so much.' 'I think the country is in bad shape when English teams keep losing in sports.' Deeper conversations invite explorations into participants' psyches and their histories: 'who they are' and 'where they are coming from'.

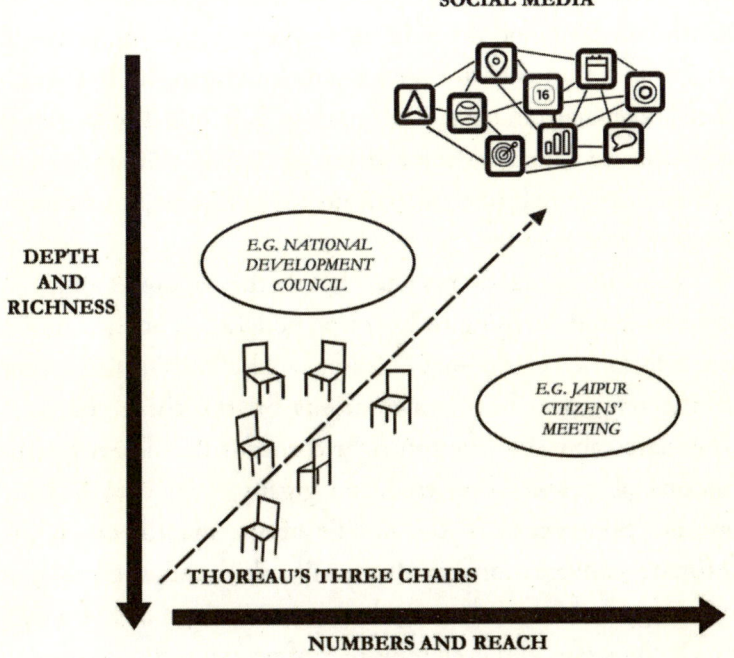

THE QUALITY OF CONVERSATIONS

Along the east-west or horizontal axis, I plot the 'reach' of conversations—i.e. the number of participants in the conversation. At one end is a person in a conversation with his own mind—like Thoreau in his solitude. Further to the right are two, then three, and on the extreme right of the horizontal axis are millions of people in the world.

Shirley Turkle has used the metaphor of Thoreau's three chairs to explain how social media is weakening the fundamental structures required for good conversations in her book *Reclaiming Conversations: The Power of Talk in a Digital Age*. I will also use Thoreau's three chairs to explain the concepts of 'richness' and 'reach' in conversations to make a map of different types of conversations.

Thoreau, sitting on his chair beside the window, looking at the pond, and listening to his own thoughts, is at the bottom and left corner of the map. Nearby, at the bottom left corner of the map, are deep conversations on the three chairs in Thoreau's cabin. On the top right corner is the Internet, with billions of people connected and gigabytes of data floating around. Somewhere in the middle of the map, between the intimate conversations in Thoreau's cabin and the millions tweeting on the Internet, are the many meetings and seminars in which dozens and even hundreds of people gather to discuss something that matters to them. Conversations in some of these meetings, such as the meeting in Jaipur described earlier, have more depth than some others, such as the meetings of the NDC, also described earlier. Therefore, meetings designed like the Jaipur meeting would be deeper down in the map, closer to conversations on Thoreau's three chairs, than to the pro forma meetings of the NDC.

There is a trade-off between the richness of conversations and their reach. Social media does give immense reach for conversations, in which millions, even billions, can be connected. However, social media is polluting the calm spaces we need

BUILDING AND CROSSING BRIDGES

for deep conversations. The intrusion of tweets, images and messages from everywhere, with our 'always active' smartphones, even when we are alone, alters the structure of the conversations in our minds. We hear more data. We cannot listen to our own thoughts.

I indulged myself one evening, after a seminar in a dark conference room in a Mumbai hotel, to sit quietly in the rooftop restaurant for dinner, and watch the sunset fading over the Arabian Sea. A young man and woman sat on the table next to mine. Then another woman joined them. Thoreau's three chairs, I thought. Except that they had the Arabian Sea and a warm sunset outside, instead of Walden Pond and snow. The waiter lit a candle on their table, brought champagne in a bucket, and poured three flutes for them. They raised their champagne flutes, looked up from their smartphones for a few seconds at each other, said 'cheers', and quickly returned to their smartphones to find out what was happening in the world elsewhere. They didn't seem interested in what was happening in each other's hearts and minds.

The election of Donald Trump as the President of the US in November 2016 shook the country. According to the Pew Research Center, 78 per cent of US citizens were connected with each other on social media in 2016. Yet, one half of the country did not know how differently and deeply the other half felt. The media had not gauged the depth and extent of citizens' mistrust in the establishment. Even professional pollsters could not predict the outcome. Some months before the US elections, Britain was shocked by the outcome of the Brexit referendum. Sixty per cent of the UK citizens were up on social media in 2015. What startled those who were opposed to Brexit was that there were so many people around them—in fact a majority—who thought very different from them. What jolted them was that they were completely unaware of the depth and extent of the misgivings within their own country, even amongst neighbours in their own communities, despite being widely connected on social media.

Refugees risking their lives, crammed on boats, to cross the Mediterranean Sea are a metaphor for the state of globalization we have reached. Now they are being shut out in Europe and the US because they are 'different people'. At first, they were more welcome. Then, deep divisions emerged within citizens of the host countries. Brexit in the UK, the election and actions of President Trump in the US, and the rise of 'alt-right' and nativist political leaders in Europe have revealed the schisms within supposedly liberal democracies.

Citizens could not understand the complexity of social and economic issues that affected their well-being. They seemed to have little faith in the establishment's explanations. The public discourse, such as it was on these issues, skimmed along shallowly in TV debates and social media. The truth could not be fathomed in this discourse. Indeed, 'alternative truths' became a common expression, and 'post-truth' was declared by the Oxford Dictionaries as the word of the year. Social media, rather than creating more harmony in society by bringing people together, seems to be creating deeper and wider divisions. This

BUILDING AND CROSSING BRIDGES

does not bode well for a liberal democracy.

There is great diversity in the world of races, religions and cultures. Therefore, people have different lenses through which they see the reality and know the truth. Democracy, with harmony amongst people, will require processes for conversations that have both reach and richness, amongst people who have different histories and points of view.

ONE FOR REFLECTION, TWO FOR CONVERSATION, THREE FOR SOCIETY

8

THE PILLARS OF THE BRIDGE: RICHNESS IN CONVERSATIONS

Conversation—respectful, engaged, reciprocal, calling forth some of our greatest powers of empathy and understanding—is the moral form of a world governed by the dignity of difference.

—Jonathan Sacks, *The Dignity of Difference*

The answer to the question 'How on Earth can we live together in harmony, with each other, and with the one Earth we share?' lies in the evolution of wider and richer conversations amongst us in which we listen deeply to people not like us.

Over the map of 'richness' and 'reach' of conversations that I introduced in the last chapter, I now project the image of a bridge with pillars that have deep foundations, and with wide and long spans. Strong and large bridges must be built across the deep and wide divisions of people, within countries and across their borders too, for a world in which all people can live harmoniously together despite their differences. These bridges will have to be built within our minds first, with 'richness' in our conversations with people not like us, before we are prepared to open physical borders and build concrete bridges that will enable us to mingle freely in a truly global world.

Bridges have two principal structures—spans to carry people across a chasm and pillars to support those spans. The spans provide the reach, while the pillars provide the strength. The deeper and wider the chasm, the deeper and stronger the pillars must be.

In this chapter, we will look at the construction of deeply set pillars for conversational bridges. In the following chapters, we will look at the architecture of spans that have width and reach, and that can carry the traffic of democratic deliberations amongst people who see the world very differently.

In the meeting between unions and employers in Mumbai, which I have described earlier in this book, it became clear that there was little trust between both the sides. I pointed out to them in the meeting that they were not listening to each other. They continued to see each other as stereotypes. There seemed to be very little connection between the *real* people behind those stereotypes.

After the meeting, I was approached by some leaders in industry and separately by some union leaders. They asked me to convene a meeting of leaders from both the sides to begin a new dialogue between them. They suggested that this should become a broad-based national movement and therefore, more persons from both the sides should be invited to join

THE PILLARS OF THE BRIDGE: RICHNESS IN CONVERSATIONS

them. There were many sceptics on both the sides, who would come to the meeting only if I, as a member of the Planning Commission, invited them.

At their first meeting in the Planning Commission, the union and management leaders recounted their disappointments with the official tripartite processes. Agreements seemed to have been reached—at least according to the records—but were not implemented. Therefore, another round of discussions would follow, but that too would turn out to be a formality with no results afterwards. Both union and management sides agreed that the process of deliberation must be changed to get better results.

Important decisions regarding the design of the dialogue process between unions and employers were taken early on. One decision was to invite some leaders of industry federations and unions in their personal capacity, though they were designated leaders within their organizations. The leaders invited were persons willing to step out of the discourse which was stuck like a gramophone record until then, and willing to listen to opposing views because they were more interested to produce better relationships between stakeholders rather than win the argument for their side. Though the leaders were persons who carried weight within 'their side', they would not be expected to automatically commit their organizations to new ideas that emerged in the dialogue. They were expected to go back to their organizations and get wider support for the new ideas.

The intention of the dialogue, it was agreed, was to build new bridges across the divide among the various stakeholder groups, even before all internal divides within the groups were resolved. It was believed that the emergence of new possibilities, created by leaders from both the sides working together on a new dialogue, would inspire fence-sitters within the stakeholder groups to come along, thus creating a movement of change. It was accepted that there may be permanent nay sayers on both the sides, but they would matter less when the movement for change would gain strength.

The objective of the process was to provide the stakeholders another platform outside the formal systems of tripartite labour conferences and the like. On this platform, they could hear each other in a new way and together develop solutions to ensure that the rights of employees are respected, while, at the same time, creating conditions to allow employers to improve the competitiveness of their enterprises. This would enable employers to develop their enterprises and generate more employment.

The dialogue amongst the stakeholders deepened steadily and grew. Very early on, the participants agreed that they would pay as much attention to the quality of their interactions as to the content of their discussions. They realized that the process was the means with which they could produce the desired outcome. If the process was not good, the outcome was unlikely to be achieved. To use another metaphor, the process was a bridge which they would cross together. If the bridge was too weak to take the burden of their contentions, it would collapse, and their dialogue would fail to reach its desired ends. Therefore, they had to pay attention to the bridge, which could

THE PILLARS OF THE BRIDGE: RICHNESS IN CONVERSATIONS

also be referred to as the 'platform' for their interactions. The words 'process' and 'platform' became interchangeable in their lexicon. Both referred to the bridge they were building and using at the same time for their deliberations about resolving contentious issues.

The two-tracked process—of patiently building the bridge while impatiently wishing to find concrete solutions to longstanding issues—proves a challenge in any project of creating a new platform or process for stakeholders to work together. The need to solve big problems, which have not been solved by other means, entices them to try the new process offered. They want the process to produce fast results to prove it works, or they abandon it. In their impatience to find solutions, they persist with the behaviours they are familiar with, and do not appreciate that it is their behaviour in meetings that they must focus on and change if they want to find solutions now. Thus, they overload the bridge too soon and it breaks. Therefore, the progress of the project must be assessed by both the progress being made in building a new and strong bridge, and progress in resolving contentious issues. Progress in resolving issues cannot get ahead of the bridge-building.

The participants in the industrial relations dialogue understood this. The bridge was the trust between them, which was strengthened in each meeting. In fact, the building of trust had become a principal objective. Trust in each other increased when they became aware of their own habitual thoughts and behaviour towards each other, which had to be changed in order to find any solution. By concentrating on the quality of trust, they paid as much attention to the bridge as to the material (the content of the discussion) they moved across it.

SURVEYING BENEATH THE WATER

Let us consider the process of building bridges. A bridge builder, having stood on a hill to survey the chasm that must be crossed, as we have done, must also examine the conditions beneath the water-line where the pillars to support the bridge will stand. Thereafter, the spans across the pillars can be envisaged to complete the bridge. Similarly, we must look beneath the water-line, and then envisage the spans.

In his poem 'Triple Bronze', Robert Frost muses about the boundaries with which we protect our own spaces—our skin to protect our bodies, walls to protect our homes, and then national boundaries to protect people like us. However, there are also mental spaces we create for our comfort and protection, around which we put up mental boundaries.[20] These mental spaces are formed by the combination of our beliefs and the lenses through which we see the world. Our beliefs and views guide us towards the people we choose to meet, the organizations we belong to, the journals we read, and the academic disciplines we study. In turn, the people we listen to, the authors we read, the organizations we belong to, and the perspectives of our disciplines, reinforce our beliefs and opinions, strengthening the implicit 'theories-in-use' at the backs of our minds. Thus,

---

[20]Ed. Lathem, Connery E., *The Poetry of Robert Frost*, Jonathan Cape, 1971.

THE PILLARS OF THE BRIDGE: RICHNESS IN CONVERSATIONS

we end up living within 'conceptually gated communities' of 'PLUs' (people like us), or in 'a world broken into fragments by narrow domestic walls' as brought out beautifully by poet Rabindranath Tagore.

Bridges between these conceptually gated communities are required to build effective coalitions and alliances for the faster development of India as well as a more harmonious world. The difficulty in building these bridges is evident from the strident cacophony of claims of righteousness of the parties on opposing sides of many conceptual divides.

A WIDENING TRUST DEFICIT

The Indian economy came through the global financial crisis of 2007–08 better off than most countries. The Indian government along with the Reserve Bank of India could steer the Indian economy safely through the turbulence. There were high hopes for growth of the Indian economy in 2009. The country had large, latent, domestic demand to fuel economic growth. It also had a very young population. There was an expectation of a sizeable 'demographic dividend' to boost and sustain the economy's growth for many years. India's GDP growth had touched 9 per cent before the global financial crisis. Economists expected it would be reaching levels of growth of 9 per cent again or even 10 per cent very soon. Instead, a policy paralysis set in and growth began to decline.

A nation wide movement arose after 2009 against corruption in the Indian State. Huge scandals, involving billions of rupees, were exposed in the allocations of telecom spectrum and in the preparations for the Commonwealth Games in Delhi. Citizens came together across class lines—middle class, poor and rich—to demand reforms of institutions and stronger anti-corruption laws. With the public in turmoil, Parliament was unable to function.

It was becoming clear to India's planners that merely economic reforms would not be sufficient for faster growth of the economy. Reforms in governance would be imperative too. Therefore, the Planning Commission undertook a 'systems' review of all the forces affecting India's economy, including forces that are not easy to quantify and, therefore, not included in economists' equations. Diverse points of view were essential to see the Indian system from many perspectives. Hence, many citizens' groups and civil society organizations, who generally do not see eye to eye with economists and find themselves shut out of economic policy decisions, were invited to participate in this exercise, along with business associations and others.

The process of collective systems thinking produced a 'systems map' which revealed the principal forces that were shaping the Indian economy, and their relationship with each other. Analysis also showed the root causes for declining growth and policy paralysis. The root cause was the enormous deficit of trust that had grown in the country. Government did not trust business. Business did not trust government. And citizens trusted neither, nor did they trust the politicians who were their representatives.

There were many issues agitating people. People were

THE PILLARS OF THE BRIDGE: RICHNESS IN CONVERSATIONS

spilling onto the streets to make themselves heard. An amusing advertisement for a popular café chain appealed for peace. In the advertisement, a young man pleads, 'Stand up for this! Stand up for that! Let us sit down and talk, yaar [i.e. friends]!'

However, there did not seem to be any place where people could sit down and talk to each other. The people's representatives were not talking to each other in the Parliament—where issues agitating people should be discussed. Whenever Parliament was convened, its members would stand up and shout slogans and the Speaker would have to adjourn the proceedings. Discussions on TV—if they could be called discussions at all—were shouting matches. The anchors of the shows would bait the participants and raise the decibel levels. And, like the mobs watching gladiatorial contests in Roman arenas, the people seemed to enjoy it—the channels with the most noise had the highest audience ratings and the most advertising revenues. 'Sit down and talk,' the young man in the advertisement had pleaded. But where should people sit down and talk to each other? And how should they talk to each other? Even in the cafés, to which the advertisements sought to attract them, they were offered free Wi-Fi so that they could use their smartphones and not have to talk to each other at all!

Several surveys, such as the Edelman Trust Barometer and the World Values Survey have reported that trust in institutions has declined in many countries around the world, not just in India. Public discourse too has degenerated everywhere, not just in India. The US media is divided into opposing camps, one supporting the Republicans and the other the Democrats.

Republicans watch Fox News. Democrats watch CNN. Therefore, the US citizens hear only one side of the issues that are troubling them—whether it is healthcare or guns control or immigration. Moreover, social media has rendered public discourse shallow, with citizens, and even the President of the US, expressing their opinions in short tweets.

People are not listening to each other all over the world, and especially not to those who have different views. Consequently, trust is declining within societies.

DISCUSSIONS, DEBATES, DELIBERATIONS AND DIALOGUES

Discussions amongst people can be conducted in many different formats. There are debates, deliberations and dialogues. The default format is the free-for-all cacophony in which everyone is yelling and no one is listening, like the melees on TV shows and in Parliament. Good debates, deliberations and dialogues have rules for their conduct that participants must follow. Moreover, since debates, deliberations and dialogues have different purposes (as we will soon see), they must follow different rules for their conduct.

A 'debate' is described by Webster's dictionary as 'a contest in which the affirmative and negative sides of a proposition are advocated by opposing speakers.' The method of adversarial debate is widely used to explore issues, whether in law courts, political assemblies or academic institutions. Debate as a method of inquiry is rooted deeply in the methods of the

THE PILLARS OF THE BRIDGE: RICHNESS IN CONVERSATIONS

Greeks, of Aristotle and Socrates. The prevalent Western version of the Socratic Method, according to Barbara Tannen, in *The Argument Culture: Stopping America's War of Words* (Ballantine Books, 1999), is clearly an adversarial debate. She says, 'An adversarial public debate is unlikely to result in opponents changing their minds. Someone who loses a debate usually attributes that loss to poor performance or to an adversary's unfair tactics.' A major problem with this approach of inquiring into issues is that when one side has been shown to have lost, and perhaps been insulted in the bargain, it becomes very difficult to arrive at a consensus between the adversaries thereafter. The Navajo Indians believe that if one ends a dispute by having a winner and a loser, one dispute may have ended but another will surely have started, because harmony will not have been restored.

Amartya Sen describes the Indian culture as argumentative in his book *The Argumentative Indian* (Penguin, 2005). However, his description of an 'argument' is different from Tannen's. According to him, an argument is not a 'war of words', which Tannen laments debates and arguments have degenerated into, in America. Sen describes an Indian tradition of argument going back to its rulers in history. He quotes the examples of Emperor Akbar in the sixteenth century, who brought people of different faiths together in his court to address the difficult problems of social harmony, and Emperor Asoka in the third century BC, who organized the third Buddhist council also bringing together people from different faiths. Asoka formulated rules of public discussion. Reasoned dialogue, according to

Asoka requires restraint in speech, so that there should be no extolment of one's own sect or disparagement of other sects. He insisted that other sects should be duly honoured in every way on all occasions. Sadly, those are not the rules followed in arguments and debates in India now. Public discourses in India have also degenerated into wars of words and gladiatorial contests for public entertainment.

The National Coalition of Dialogue and Deliberation (NCDD) in the US gathers descriptions of processes adopted in many countries for citizens to discuss matters that concern them. Explaining these processes on NCDD's website (ncdd.org), Sandy Heierbacher, NCDD's convener, defines 'deliberation' as a process which 'promotes the use of critical reasoning and logical argument in decision-making.' 'Instead of decision-making by power, coercion, or hierarchy, deliberative decision-making emphasizes the examination of facts and arguments and the weighing of pros and cons of various options,' she says. This description of a 'deliberation' conforms more closely with the rules Emperor Asoka had laid down for discussions, rather than the rules of an adversarial 'debate' that have become prevalent in public discourse in America, in India, and elsewhere too.

Heierbacher distinguishes 'dialogue' from 'deliberation'. Dialogue, she says, is a process that allows people to share their perspectives and experiences with one another about difficult issues. 'Dialogue is not about judging, weighing or making decisions, but about understanding and learning. Dialogue dispels stereotypes, builds trust and enables people to be open to perspectives that are very different to their own.'

Let us stack up the four methods of discussion we have examined: a cacophony (when there is no method to subdue the madness), debates, deliberations and dialogues. In a cacophony, people are only speaking and not listening. In debates, the opponents listen to each other's arguments carefully with a view to trip each other. Like boxers are attentive to their opponents' moves, they listen carefully to each other's words so that they can find any openings for their counter thrusts. Deliberations demand that people listen more deeply, to understand others' points of view, and to enquire into why they think the way they do, rather than to immediately find what is wrong in their view. Deliberation requires people to listen deeply to 'why' people think the way they do. Dialogue requires that people listen even more deeply, to understand 'who' the other person really is, behind the stereotypes in our minds about them.

The four methods of discussion are distinguished from each other by the depth of listening required in them.

We are losing the discipline of listening to others. We teach students, in schools and colleges, how to be better debaters and the best ones are honoured. Leaders in organizations are taught the skills of public speaking—of getting their points across to people effectively. On social media, we must learn to make sharp, attention-receiving statements in 140 characters. It is always about how to speak effectively to be heard, not about how to listen to others.

His Holiness the Dalai Lama says the arts of listening and dialogue must become parts of the curriculum in schools to reduce the level of violence in the world. In his address to the university in Dharamshala (of which I am the Chancellor), at its first convocation in February 2013, he said:

> I believe that the notion and practice of dialogue can and should be taught (to students) in schools, just as we teach them to appreciate democracy. We can train students to debate different views. In this way, the concepts of dialogue and resolving conflict non-violently will be instilled in them. Consequently, they will become used to the idea that whenever they are faced with a conflict, the best and most practical way of resolving it is through dialogue, not violence. Violence means one side has victory while the other side suffers defeat, but that's not realistic in today's world where everyone's interests are so intertwined. To solve a problem, you must appreciate what is at stake for your opponents. You have to take care of their interests as well as you can and, in that light, try to find a solution.

'Fundamentally,' says the Dalai Lama, 'Human beings are all the same: we all want happiness and do not want suffering. Appreciating this sameness is crucial to respecting and understanding other people and to developing compassion and kindness towards them.' 'Fundamentalisms, we should never forget,' explains Jonathan Sacks in *The Dignity of Difference: How to Avoid the Clash of Civilizations* (Continuum, 2002), 'Can be economic or scientific as well as religious. Without a moral vision, we will fail. And that vision, to be shared, can only emerge from conversation—from talking to one another

THE PILLARS OF THE BRIDGE: RICHNESS IN CONVERSATIONS

and listening to one another across boundaries of class, income, race, and faith.'

Such conversations in which people listen to each other deeply must happen in many forums, formal and informal, in which people connect with each other at deeper levels to build bridges across their differences.

SO MUCH TO BUY; WHAT'S THE NEED FOR NEWS

9

THE SPANS OF THE BRIDGE
PART A: THE MEDIA

Were it left to me to decide whether we should have a government without newspapers, or newspapers without a government, I should not hesitate a moment to prefer the latter. Our liberty depends on the freedom of the press, and that cannot be limited without being lost.

—Thomas Jefferson

A bridge to carry heavy traffic must be built upon strong pillars firmly embedded in the ground beneath the water. Dialogic processes, with deep listening, provide good foundations and strong pillars for bridges to connect people with deep-rooted differences.

We will now examine the construction of spans across the pillars to enable the bridge to carry millions of people, back and forth, in democratic deliberations amongst them. We will look at the structures of the media, and the manner in which they are being altered by business values overtaking traditional journalism values, and by growth of social media.

WHAT MONEY SHOULDN'T BUY

The completely unexpected victory of Donald Trump as the President of the US threw mud in the face of mainstream media, which it has not yet been able to wipe off. In a turn-of-the-year introspection in CNN's Reliable Sources show on New Year's Day 2017, Carolyn Ryan, Senior Editor for Politics in the *New York Times*, Michael Oreskes, Head of News for NPR, and Kathleen Carrol, former editor with the *Associated Press*, discussed citizens' increasing mistrust of institutions in general, and the media in particular. They wondered why the media 'could not get it'. Why couldn't all political polls and political pundits in the mainstream media understand what was going on in the country? They worried that the mainstream media was becoming increasingly irrelevant in public affairs. Carolyn Ryan was troubled that the media was paying too much attention to listening to its own readers and viewers, and too little to listening to people in general. The fundamental questions were what role should serious media play in society and whether it was capable of playing that role any longer.

Listening to that discussion, I had a sense of déjà vu, with a recollection of another discussion on the role of the media. This was at the Aspen Institute's seminar on the Challenges of Global Capitalism in Aspen, Colorado, in July 2002. It was conducted by philosopher Michael Sandel, author of *Democracy's Discontent: America in Search of a Public Philosophy*

(1998) and the bestseller *What Money Can't Buy: The Moral Limits of Markets* (2012). In the seminar, Jerry Levin, CEO of Time Warner, chaired a discussion on the role of media.

Many participants expressed their anguish at the 'dumbing down' of discourse on mainstream media. Discussions on TV had deteriorated into gladiatorial contests, such as the hugely successful American show at that time, *Crossfire*. The participants asked, 'How citizens would be engaged with the deeper issues of their societies if all they saw and read in the media was designed only to entertain them? Did the media not have a responsibility, as a pillar of democracy, to engage and educate citizens about these issues?'

Presaging Carolyn Ryan's concern in the New Year's Day CNN discussion, Levin explained why the media must focus on the demands of its readers and viewers. He said the media as a business, and a good business must give its customers what they wanted. If they wanted more entertainment, then the media must give them good entertainment. If the media did not give its customers what they wanted, it would go out of business, he warned.

A participant in the Aspen Seminar said that society could not allow business leaders to get away with the justification that they were giving people what they wanted. 'Many people want hard drugs,' she said. 'There is a lot of money to be made by supplying hard drugs to these customers. Could a business that supplied hard drugs be defended on the principle that it was giving people what they wanted? Just as sellers of drugs are declared criminals, all business leaders must be held responsible for the bad effects of their products and services on the lives of people,' she declared. Moreover, the participants felt, the media has a special place in democratic societies. The media is given the freedom, as a conscience-keeper of a society's values, to comment freely on social issues and to criticize all other institutions, including governments in power. The media must not become a business like any other business, they insisted.

THE DUMBING DOWN OF PUBLIC DISCOURSE

More recently, the angst about the diminishing role of the media in shaping public discourse was very evident in 'Forum 2000', which was held in Prague in October 2016. 'Forum 2000' was established in 2000 by Vaclav Havel, the playwright-philosopher who led Czechoslovakia's peaceful Velvet Revolution against Soviet rule, for thought-leaders to periodically meet and reflect on the state of democracy in the world. The concern with the role of the media had increased between the Aspen Seminar in July 2002 and the Forum 2000 in October 2016 because of the roll-out of social media in the interim. Social media has changed the character of the media. It has dumbed down public discourse.

In a special discussion at Forum 2000 on 'Is the media still setting the agenda?' Thomas Kent, President of Radio Free Europe, Petr Dvorak, Director General of Czech TV, and Per Nylhom, a well-known Danish commentator and writer, observed that the 'serious' media was setting the agenda only within limited groups of 'people like us'. The public thinks that serious media represents only the elite, whereas social media has democratized agenda-setting.

Social media was hailed as the technical saviour of democracy in the Arab Spring. It seemed to have provided the means for citizens from outside the political establishment to overcome the power of autocracies. Barack Obama used social media to assist him against democracy's establishment (professional politicians, political parties and the big money that supports them). However, disillusionment with social media ran through the discussions at Forum 2000.

In an interview in October 2016 with *The World Post*, Wael Ghonim, the Internet activist who helped spawn the Arab Spring in Egypt with his Facebook posts, said that the structure of social media promotes 'mobocracy', not democracy and that it '...brings together people with common passions irrespective of whether the information they share is the truth, rumour or lies.' He insists that 'While once social media was seen as a liberating means to speak truth to power, now the issue is how to speak truth to social media.'

'It all boils down to money,' speakers at Forum 2000 lamented. Advertisers provide the money that media needs to run. Media owners pander to advertisers. TRPs on TV and eyeballs and clicks on social media have become the measures of success of media businesses. On social media, customers don't pay for content, and social media owners don't pay producers of content. Citizens post videos, make comments and report 'news'. The more shocking these posts, the more attention they attract, and more advertisers can be charged. Thus, a vicious circle has formed, like a tightening noose, and we have entered a 'Post-truth' era in the media and in public discourse, with quality of the content and the truth gasping for air.

Money should not be able to buy people's votes, but it does. This is why reform of the funding of elections and political parties is imperative for the health of democracy. Money should not be able to buy people's minds, which it does when the media becomes a business like any other. Therefore, the reform of media institutions—their funding and their ownership—has become imperative for the survival of democracy.

Economist Albert O. Hirschman saw the contradiction between institutions of capitalism and democracy building up 50 years ago. He observed in his book *Exit, Voice, and Loyalty* (Harvard University Press, 1970) that the more attention business managers pay to listening to their customers and the better they get at it, the less capable they become to hear the voices of citizens in society.

Hirschman pointed out that Milton Friedman, who famously decreed that 'the business of business must only be business', had expressed his difficulty in accepting the notion that people should desire to express their views to make them prevail. Friedman describes people's desire to be heard as a resort to 'cumbrous political channels'. He would much rather they resort to 'efficient market mechanisms' and use their money rather than their mouths to make their opinions known.

Business corporations in general will have to change the principles by which they operate for democracy (and indeed for humanity) to survive. The business of business must not be only business. The purpose of a business corporation, regardless of the sector—media, manufacturing or services—cannot be only the production of profits and financial value for investors. Corporations must be governed with other values: caring for the conditions of the environment and communities in which they operate. Just as democratic governments are expected to be accountable to citizens, corporations must be accountable to citizens too, not only to their customers and investors.

The media has a special place in democratic societies that other businesses do not have. The media must be free to hold up a mirror to citizens to let them see the ugly side of their society along with its beauty. It must tell citizens and their leaders not what they like to hear, but what they must. When Mark Zuckerberg considers that Facebook is not merely a technology company, but a publisher of news—a question he appeared to be pondering over after the controversies about 'alternative facts' posted on Facebook that went viral during the last US Presidential elections—he will have to face up to the vital role that media must play in shaping democratic societies.

CONSUMERS AND CITIZENS

The Internet and the World Wide Web have proven to be a boon for consumers. They can choose from a great variety of products and services offered on websites, which are also accessible free of cost from smartphones anywhere. Competition among sellers is driving down prices for consumers.

Every year, when I go to see my daughter, who lives in

Oakland in the Bay Area of California, I visit Walden Pond Books, one of the few remaining independent booksellers in the US. Most independent booksellers did not survive the onslaught of the big chain stores such as Barnes & Noble and Borders. But the big chains are now struggling against a tsunami started by the Internet.

The Bay Area has been a vortex of anti-establishment movements for over 50 years. Upsurges for the rights of gays, blacks, labour and many other causes were born, or were given energy at their birth, by people in Oakland and the other towns around it. An independent bookstore in Oakland can be expected to carry books that question established views. Walden Pond Books never disappoints me. Every year, I return with several books whose authors look differently at the world than celebrated authors and journalists whose views direct mainstream thinking about the forces shaping the world.

The Internet was not born in the Bay Area, but its enormous power was grown by the energies of many start-ups in Silicon Valley, a few miles from Oakland. The world's largest makers of chips, computers and software; owners of the world's largest social media platforms; and giants of e-commerce have made the area the global centre of the Internet revolution.

The popular view of the Internet as a democratizing and empowering force sits very well with the anti-establishment spirit of the Bay Area. Young people in jeans, starting up businesses in garages, are upending the world of established businesses—books, music, hotels, retail and taxi businesses… the list is getting longer.

THE SPANS OF THE BRIDGE

Sitting in a small, independent bookstore in Oakland that may not last against the global forces for change emanating only a few miles away, I found a book with an intriguing title: *The Internet is NOT the Answer* (Atlantic Monthly Press, 2015). The answer to what, I wondered? I browsed through its pages. The author, Andrew Keen, insists that the Internet is creating an undemocratic concentration of power. It is making us smart consumers, but ill-informed citizens.

The Internet may be a boon for consumers, but so far it is neither making the world better for citizens, nor making us consumers into better citizens. Internet platforms have made information abundantly available for free. It has become an ocean of 'water, water everywhere, but not enough good water to drink.' A lot of chatter, but what is the insight? A lot of noise, but what is the signal?

The Internet, social media and mobile phones bombard us with millions of bits of information, messages and tweets. It is difficult for anyone to keep in touch with everyone and everything. If we are connected, we suffer from an 'attention deficit disorder'. Coping strategies are: remain 'on' all the time; pay shallow attention to many things and choose the many we wish to follow from the millions we can. All these strategies make a deeper understanding of other persons impossible.

Remaining 'on' all the time with shallow attention reduces the depth at which we are with others. People meet to have coffee together; but everyone is looking into their smartphones, and not at each other. People at a business meeting keep one eye on their smartphone or iPad on the table, and the other to dip in and out of what is happening in the room. Internet and social media have vast 'reach', but staying connected reduces the 'richness' of the conversations among people.

The third coping strategy—of choosing websites, tweeters and Facebook friends one will follow, as perforce one must—makes us stay with people we like because they are like us. We understand what they say easily. If we have to make an extra effort to understand something or someone, we just shut them out. There is no time to reflect. Thus, we get locked within 'conceptually gated communities'. Across the walls are others in their own resonance chambers like we are, hearing what they like, and listening to who they like.

A 2014 Pew Research and Rutgers University Report reveals that social media actually stifles debates between people of different opinions. It reports that the millennial 'selfie' generation has lower levels of trust of others than previous generations. Only 19 per cent of millennials (18–33-year-olds) trust others compared with 31 per cent of Gen Xers and 40 per cent of boomers (who grew up without the benefits of smartphones and social media).

Prolific users of social media are self-absorbed. Surveying many studies, Keen says the conclusion is that 'communications are degenerating into the immediate, the intimate, and above all, the self-obsessed.' Facebook urges us to reveal our 'true' selves to others. Sheryl Sandberg, Facebook's Chief Operating Officer, says that 'You cannot be on Facebook without being your true authentic self.' Mark Zuckerberg, Facebook's Chief Executive Officer, says that 'Having two identities for yourself is an example of a lack of integrity.'

The reality is that Facebook and other web-based communication platforms make it very easy for us to live many parallel lives. We do not know the real identity of the other person that we are so attracted to. Many Internet encounters end in tragedies when the protagonists are revealed in real life as charlatans, rapists and sadistic murderers. On the Internet it is becoming more, not less, difficult to know who the other person is.

Further, we can easily live in a world of make-believe on the Internet. Children play games in virtual worlds, imagining themselves as superheroes (or powerful villains). Forays into the virtual world can become like addictive trips on drugs. The inventors and sellers of these addictive games make a lot of money. A new, popular game takes people one step further away from reality: the viewer need not play the game himself; just watch others playing their virtual games! Thus, people float even further away for long periods into make-believe spaces with neither time nor interest to smell real roses.

Charles Handy, a thought leader about the state of the world and its future, says in his latest book:

> Social media creates what some have called a dissatisfied narcissism as we endlessly seek an elusive perfection, like wearing all our clothes at once. The social media knows no deference and carries with it no sense of responsibility, no awareness of its impact on others. What is happening right now becomes dominant, skewing our priorities, neglecting

the longer-term impact. A world of instantaneous messaging, simultaneous multi-viewing of data on demand but without analysis, can, if we are not careful, lead to a shallow and self-centred take on the world, a Twittering world where no one has the concentration or the time to take in more than a paragraph.[21]

CONNECTING US, AND ALSO DIVIDING US

The principal thrust of new technology in social media businesses is to provide better algorithms that can determine what each person likes and give him/her more of that. If we like some views, social media will give us more of the same. It does not waste any of its business resources (and our time) by offering us anything different. This is smart business. But it makes human beings into increasingly passive consumers rather than responsible citizens with inquiring minds who have doubts and questions and are competent to make their own choices.

The Oxford Dictionaries Word of the Year 2016 is 'post-truth'. Post-truthism in public discourse has been growing rapidly with the expansion of social media. The political and societal implications of it were realized with a thud with the shock of Donald Trump's completely unexpected election as President of the US in November last year. 'In the end, the finger pointing got to Facebook's boss, Mark Zuckerberg',

---

[21]Handy, Charles, *The Second Curve: Thoughts on Reinventing Society*, Random House, 2015.

THE SPANS OF THE BRIDGE

The Guardian reported on 20 November 2016. Mark Zuckerberg has set up a News Partnership team to deal with the problem and Facebook will also develop new algorithms to filter out 'non truths' in public postings.

We must listen to people with different beliefs, who are not like us, to bridge deep boundaries that are even dividing people of the same colour and the same religion within countries. The Brexit referendum and the election of Donald Trump have exposed these divisions in nations that have so far been proud of their democratic character and the quality of their free press.

The combination of technology with journalism has created a philosophical problem that technology alone cannot resolve. On the one hand, technology algorithms are expected to become even more efficient at giving us only what we already like. On the other hand, Facebook's CEO says new algorithms will be developed to direct us to also listen to people who are not like us and who we may not like. What should the algorithm shut out and what should it bring to our attention? Who will give the machine the rules to follow? What are this person's values and beliefs?

Google is a blessing for us as consumers of information. It provides us access to a wealth of information for free. Facebook and other social media platforms enable people to connect with others very easily for free. The theory is that this unprecedented ease of finding out and of connecting with each other using the Internet platforms must make us better citizens of the world. However, rather than making us smarter and rather than uniting us, the proliferation of information may be making us dumber and dividing us further.

Citizens want journalists to tell only the truth: to report the facts undistorted by their personal values. This would be impossible. Journalists are human beings too. Like all human beings, they acquire lenses through which they see the world: lenses that are shaped by their own histories, the cultures of the communities in which they have been brought up and their education. Philosopher Hilary Putnam (*The Collapse of the Fact/Value Dichotomy and Other Essays*, 2004) has argued that the distinction between factual claims and value judgements is positively harmful when identified with a dichotomy between the 'objective' and the purely 'subjective'. The 'facts' journalists can see are unavoidably coloured by their personal lenses and their subjective values.

Journalists who want to report important facts to the public have two dilemmas. One is the age-old dilemma mentioned before about the impossibility of separating their own values from their account of the facts—of separating subjectivity from objectivity in social affairs. Even as they write, they will apply adjectives before nouns to make their account of the facts interesting to their readers. The adjectives they choose accord with their views about the person or place they are writing about. For instance, is Mumbai a dynamic city or a decaying city? Is Donald Trump a strong leader or an unreliable leader?

The second dilemma for journalists is a more recent one created by the conversion of media into a business like any other, and also by the rapid proliferation of social media. Journalists need to be heard to be able to convey truths. Social media has made it more difficult for reflective commentators to be heard. To use an analogy, once upon a time crooners and balladeers could gently sing words that moved us, with a piano or a guitar in company. Today, singers must yell and curse to be heard above the din created by the percussion blasting through amplifiers. Similarly, quiet commentary in the media is not noticed by the public. Tweets by celebrities about their birthday parties, and their views about anything and everything, get most attention. The principal competition to them for attention on social media is trolls who curse, spew hate and spread canards. As journalists lamented in Forum 2000 that serious journalists and writers do not get attention in popular media. They are able to set the agenda only within limited groups. The masses are not listening to them. And they are not listening to the masses.

DOING THE RIGHT THING

The quality and tone of public discourse in the modern world has become too shallow. TV and social media have become the most ubiquitous means for public discourse. The objective of producers of TV debates is to increase the numbers of viewers so that more advertisements can be sold. Therefore, debates have degenerated into entertainment, with big fights between participants that provide the public with hardly any education about the issue being debated. A dialogue, in which the participants listen to each other, rather than put each other down, is boring, according to TV producers. Viewers will switch off the channel; advertising revenues will be lost.

Maria Popova, the Bulgarian writer, said in her commencement address in 2016 at the University of Pennsylvania's Annenberg School of Communication:

> As long as we feed people buzz, we cannot expect their minds to produce symphonies. Never let the temptation of marketable mediocrity and easy cynicism rob you of the chance to ennoble public life and enlarge the human spirit—because we need that badly today, and because you need it badly for your soul.[22]

So what should a writer, who is concerned about the dumbing down of public discourse, and is not willing to go with the herd, do?

When I was in college over 50 years ago, I participated in a debate. The subject was Bertrand Russel's famous comment: 'I would rather be Red than dead.' I got the subject slightly wrong. I thought it was, 'I would rather be read than dead.' Those who had got it right spoke about the pros and cons of communism. Some went deeper to debate whether one should give up one's convictions to survive and join the Reds if to oppose them would be fatal.

Mistaking red for read, my concern was with the dilemma of a person who wants to change the tide. He must speak up

---

[22]'On the Soul-Sustaining Necessity of Resisting Self-Comparison and Fighting Cynicism: A Commencement Address—Brain Pickings'—https://www.brainpickings.org/

THE SPANS OF THE BRIDGE

and be heard to have any influence on public values. However, if by being heard, he risks being permanently silenced before he can influence any change, then what is the use of speaking up? On the other hand, if he chooses to conform so that he can survive to be heard, what will he say? What will become of his own values?

Donald Trump is heard widely because he tells many people what they want to hear. He speaks in a language that shocks and frequently tweets what his supporters, as well as those who do not agree with him, cannot help but hear. He is heard by all above the background noise.

Eight years ago, the new editor of a newspaper for whom I had been writing a monthly column for many years, told me that competition from social media was compelling his paper to change its tone and style. He said the subjects of my pieces were too serious, and the style too calm, for the younger readers that his paper must attract. Could I write about the more mundane concerns of these young readers? Could I make my language louder and shriller, he asked, to appeal to them?

There were some truths about our society and ourselves that I felt must be said, even to young people, even if they do not want to hear them. Also, I could not bring myself to exaggerate and curse just to be read. So I declined to distort my writing. I lost access to a large pool of potential readers that I could have had if I chose to conform to the tide. Did I do the right thing?

A principal cause for the challenge to liberal democracy from rising authoritarianism and populism in many countries is the perception amongst the 99 per cent that the 1 per cent is colluding with their governments to make rules that serve them. They are corrupting institutions to serve their narrow interests. Political parties, large corporations and mainstream media are all tarred in the public mind with the brush of moral corruption. The solution for the decay of institutions cannot be another institution above them all to make them more honest. That is because it cannot be ensured that this institution will not be corrupted too when it is led by similar people.

The solution has to be the awakening of the moral consciences of leaders of political parties, business corporations and the media. They, and the institutions they lead, must serve the needs of citizens and society, and not just their own personal needs of power, profit and popularity. To have the courage to speak truth to power, and also to be heard above the din, have become the principal challenges of our times for good journalists and citizens who want to make the world better for everyone.

10

THE SPANS OF THE BRIDGE
PART B: DEMOCRATIC DELIBERATIONS

The romance of democracy is that somehow the result will come out the way you want, but everything we know about democracy is that the result comes out the way the people want.

—John Mueller

Donald Trump's trump card, with which he defeated his formidable political opponents in the Republican primaries and Hillary Clinton too, was that he is an anti-establishment 'un-politician'. His unexpectedly large following in the US has alarmed the world. In India, the other huge democracy, the Aam Aadmi Party (AAP), running on the plank of a new, people's politics against the political establishment, made a clean sweep in 2015 Delhi state elections. Trump and Arvind Kejriwal (the founder of AAP) are completely different persons who tapped into the rising discontent of citizens in two separate democracies.

IT IS WONDERFUL TO BE TOGETHER AGAIN

CITIZENS AND THEIR DISCONTENT

The Economist reports that a quarter of Americans born since 1980 believe democracy is a bad form of government.[23] Citizens of European countries are also becoming disenchanted with democracy's institutions. Sophie Kleeman reports that according to the Institute for Democracy and Electoral Assistance, the voter rate reflects the frustrations with democracy in the Czech Republic and has followed a downward trend. From a 96 per cent turnout rate in the 1990 parliamentary elections—the first following the Revolution—the voter turnout has dropped in every proceeding year to 62.6 per cent in the parliamentary elections in 2010, and to around 35 per cent in the recent regional elections in 2016. Kleeman reports that the reason for this, according to Jiri Pehe, a political analyst and former adviser to Vaclav Havel, is an intense distrust of the government and the political parties who control it.[24]

Diversity amongst people in the world and amongst people within countries too, provides stimuli for creativity and innovation. However, diversity also brings challenges. People have different histories, different cultures, different concerns, and even their dreams are different. Democracy requires that

---

[23]'America's Best Hope', *The Economist*, 5 November 2016 http://www.economist.com/news/leaders/21709540-why-we-would-cast-our-hypothetical-vote-hillary-clinton-americas-best-hope

[24]Kleeman, Sophie, 'Czech Voter Turnout: No Belief, No Vote', *The New Presence*, 2016. http://www.pritomnost.cz/en/czech-politics/379-czech-voter-turnout-no-belief-no-vote

they respect each other's histories, understand each other's concerns and share and combine their dreams to shape their future together. The purpose of democratic institutions must be to enable people who are not like each other to overcome their historical divisions and intermingle more freely in spite of their differences. This must be the path for the evolution of better democratic institutions within countries, and also between countries (such as the EU project, and the institutions of the UN).

Democracies require architecture of institutions. Some institutions provide the vertical pillars. Other institutions provide the lateral binders that give strength and stability to the democratic structure. In the popular discourse about democracy, and while spreading around the idea of democracy that the West, especially the US, has made its mission, too much attention has been given to the vertical institutions required for people to elect their leaders, and too little to the lateral institutions required to create harmony amongst diverse people.

Universal franchise, elections and political parties fighting each other to win elections are institutions that enable a society to determine who is in the majority and has the right to govern. The problem with majoritarian democracy is that it is not designed to find solutions for complex problems with many points of view. A government with a majority, especially a large one, can become as authoritarian as a dictatorial one. It can deny minorities their rights for their views to be considered while framing laws and resolving contentious issues. The people have spoken once; that should be enough. Now, they must leave it to the government in power. A government can justify the exclusion of the minority because it was elected by a majority.

However, by excluding the views of the many that did not vote for it—and quite often these may not even be the majority in first-past-the-post elections—a government reduces its own effectiveness. Those dissatisfied with the governments' decisions go to courts wherever courts are independent, like in India. However, courts are not set up to find policy solutions to complex problems and must interpret the laws as written. In India, ministers of the government have begun to complain that India's courts are venturing into matters of governance, which they should not. This is a sign that something is missing in India's democracy.

When problems are complex, with many interacting forces and several contending stakeholders, good governance requires effective methods for people's participation. Referendums of the entire electorate give an illusion of good democracy—that the people have been consulted. Since the opinions of masses of people must be swayed, politicians on both sides of the referendum run populist campaigns appealing to the basest of instincts. Whereas, when the issue is complex, voters should be educated about what they are voting for. And then, when a small majority determines how all must go (52 per cent versus 48 per cent for Brexit), referendums become yet another example of the problem with majoritarian democracy rather than a good solution.

DISCORD WITHIN DEMOCRACY

Healthy democracies need intermediate processes that lie between the open public sphere of civil society and the media on one side, and the formal, constitutionally established decision-making institutions, like parliaments and courts, on the other side. A free public sphere can raise issues. Social media has made it even freer. However, it cannot resolve them because people are not listening to each other. The formal institutions of democracy have become overburdened, as in India, because issues raised in the public sphere are not predigested by intermediate processes and institutions.

A selection of formats of meetings for bringing people together, from across the continuum of richness and reach, has to be combined into processes for democratic deliberation, in the space between the open public sphere and formal government institutions. These processes must adhere to some basic principles of inclusive, deliberative democracy. James Fishkin, professor of communication and political science at Stanford University, describes three principles in his book, *When the People Speak: Deliberative Democracy and Public Consultation*. He says a good process must fulfil three norms: political equality, deliberation and mass participation.[25]

The first norm, political equality, requires that all participants are considered equal in the deliberations. Those who have more—power, wealth or education—must not

---

[25] Fishkin, James S., *When the People Speak: Deliberative Democracy & Public Consultation*, Oxford University Press, 2009.

overpower the voices of others. This is not easy because we are habituated to defer to them.

The second norm, deliberation, demands that people have the required information, that they listen to other points of view, and that they are able to advocate their own views too without being intimidated by others. The conversations must be 'rich' in content, and in understanding of issues of others.

The third norm, mass participation, requires reach for many to be engaged—perhaps too many to enable richness in the deliberations.

Humanity's aspirations are reaching much higher than they were at the time of Athenian democracy. The processes of democratic discussion that Athenians used, which for a long time have inspired Western democracies, are now considered faulty. They emphasized deliberation, but did not meet the requirements of political equality and mass participation. For instance, women and slaves were excluded from participation.

The founders of the US Constitution were acutely aware of the need for suitable processes for democratic deliberation. Such processes would be necessary to implement their vision of 'government *of* the people, *for* the people, and *by* the people'. James Madison (the fourth President of the US, hailed as the 'Father of the Constitution' and the key champion of the United States Bill of Rights) described what was required and the difficulties in devising a good process, in the *Federalist Papers*. Madison wrote in *The Federalist* No. 55: 'Had every Athenian citizen been a Socrates, every Athenian assembly would still have been a mob.' Thereby, he pointed out the need for a good process for deliberations amongst people, no matter how intelligent all of them may be.

In *The Federalist* No. 10, Madison wrote about the need for taking 'raw' opinions from people and 'refining' them in bodies of elected representatives. His federalist ideas were opposed by the Anti-Federalists, who said that in a true democracy every citizen must have the right to be consulted and to participate in the process of decision-making. They advocated 'direct democracy' rather than the indirect participation of citizens in deliberations only through their elected representatives. The Anti-Federalists envisioned a 'mass democracy' rather than the 'deliberative democracy' that Madison propounded.

Madison foresaw problems in a mass democracy in which every citizen participated in decision-making. Would the citizens be well-informed about the issues at stake? Would they be able to set aside sufficient time while they were busy earning their livelihoods to understand the issues?

The problems with direct democracy have become evident in the referendum for Brexit in 2016. All the people who voted did not have all the facts. In a discussion in New York in 2004 about the condition of democracy in the world, a woman from California bemoaned the deterioration of democracy in her state into a series of direct ballots on various issues. Each of these was explained either in thick documents that nobody had time to read, or in contentious, partisan media debates that illuminated nothing more than the hate the opposing parties had for each other. She said that it was a fallacy to think that voters who had been to university (she herself had a PhD) were 'educated' about the issues they were expected to vote on. The processes of public debate were failing to educate the people about these issues and hence, all votes, even of the so-called educated elite, were merely an expression of their personal prejudices. In that way, California, she felt, was no different to India in that people, whether educated or not, voted according to their identities and their prejudices.

Madison's solution, which has been incorporated into the US Constitution, was a structure of institutions to which citizens would elect representatives. These representatives would have the time for deliberation, and the expectation was that they would consider all facts and deliberate calmly amongst themselves. They would be able to arrive at much better decisions, on behalf of the citizens, than the citizens would be able to themselves.

However, it does not work that way always. There are complications when representatives meet to deliberate and take collective decisions together. On the one hand, representatives are expected to accurately represent those who voted them. On the other, they are expected to understand the points of view of other voters who have elected other representatives, and then decide collectively. In other words, in representative democracies, the representatives are expected to change their minds when they consider all points of view. They are accused of betraying their voters if their votes in the chambers do not conform to the views of their voters. There would appear to be sufficient justification to recall such open-minded representatives and to elect others who will faithfully adhere to the prejudices of their voters.

The dilemma of representation versus openness to deliberation within elected bodies has altered the character of the institutions that Madison and others envisaged to enable better deliberation in democracies. The Electoral College was envisaged as a body of persons chosen by voters who would deliberate amongst themselves and choose, on behalf of all their voters collectively, the best candidate to put up. Whereas, in practice, all members of Electoral Colleges merely vote as they have been assigned to when they are elected. The raw and often prejudiced opinions of the masses are totalled up through chambers in which there is hardly any deliberation, into a final vote. Thus, democracy has become a process of aggregation rather than deliberation.

If representatives were to change their minds after hearing the views of others and after deliberation in the chambers, they must explain to their constituents why they did so. Otherwise, as mentioned before, their supporters will feel betrayed. In order to ensure that citizens understand the trade-offs and the benefits of a decision that they had not originally favoured, they will have to be better informed and engaged with the issues.

In his book *The Price of Civilization: Economics and Ethics after the Fall* (2011), Jeffrey Sachs, director of the Earth Institute at Columbia University, laments that in today's America there is little systematic public deliberation and the public's views are not taken seriously in the political process. He says that policy decisions are being adopted behind the backs of the public, often in direct contradiction of public opinion. Donald

Trump was carried to the top by a wave of resentment of the US citizens against elite policy-makers and politicians who, citizens believe, do not understand them, and whose arguments citizens cannot understand. A large trust deficit has emerged between democracy's formal Establishment and the people, in the US, and in Europe too, where 'populist' leaders are rising up on an anti-Establishment wave.

Michael Rabinder James observed the following in *Deliberative Democracy and the Plural Polity*, University of Kansas Press:

> For over a decade, the idea of deliberative democracy has attracted the attention of political theorists. The idea presents democracy, the rule of the people, not simply as a process in which citizens vote according to their pre-existing political preferences. Instead deliberative democrats envision citizens engaged in spirited discussions that inform and transform their political preferences before they step into the voting booth. Such discussions should, at minimum, allow citizens to obtain better information about which policies will best satisfy their individual or common interests. But more important, democratic discussion should go beyond gathering information to include dialogues aimed at understanding other participants' situations, beliefs, and interests, along with vigorous debates meant to assess the desirability of proposed measures. More precisely such discussions should encourage citizens and their representatives to

justify the measures they favour while criticising those they reject. The process should, ideally, proceed under conditions that all participants can accept as fair, thus mitigating the danger that more powerful participants will unfairly force others to alter their beliefs, interests, or preferences.[26]

Methods must be found to engage citizens, thoughtfully, with issues that matter to them. How should raw public opinions be gathered from diverse constituents of a democratic society, and what should be the design of processes for their refinement? These are critical issues in designing processes for democratic deliberation in the twenty-first century.

DELIBERATIVE DEMOCRACY

The liberal democratic order is under a grave threat because we have not been listening to the people outside our physically gated, as well as conceptually gated communities. Yet, they have been speaking to us in many ways. First it was the 'Occupy Wall Street' movement. Then it was Donald Trump and Bernie Sanders, rallying the people against the political and corporate establishment in the US. Then thousands of people began arriving in boats on the shores of Europe. And in June 2016, a majority in Britain said they wanted to get out of the EU. A few days later, thousands of people defied the government

---

[26]Michael, James R., *Deliberative Democracy and the Plural Polity*, Lawrence KS: University Press of Kansas, 2004.

THE SPANS OF THE BRIDGE

and the police in Kashmir in India to mourn at the funeral of a young militant. The startling result of the US Presidential election in November 2016 was another warning. There are more rumblings of discontent, with politics, as usual, from both the Left and the Right (such as the increasing strength of the Five Star movement in Italy, the rise of extreme right-wing parties in Austria and the Netherlands, and pronouncement of President Rodrigo Duterte in the Philippines) that are threatening liberal democratic societies in Europe and Asia.

These developments have shocked 'people like us' who thought that the history of systems of governance had ended with the collapse of the Soviet Union and the victory of (US dominated) ideas of democracy and free markets. They are 'reflections of, and expression of, the real protest about the deep inequalities of the world-system that are so politically central to our times.'[27]

Inequality has increased along with globalization and financialization of economies. Combined with inequality is a smouldering sense of unfairness, and an impression that those who have do not even care about those left behind; and that the 'haves' even believe they have obtained their wealth and power because they merit it and that those who are left behind are culturally inferior. There seem to be a million mutinies now, with perceptions of deep-rooted unfairness in established economic and political systems fuelling protests in many parts

---

[27] Wallerstein, Immanuel, *World Systems Analysis: An Introduction*, Duke University Press, 2004.

of the world, some peaceful and many violent.

It would disturb 'people like us' as the core ideas that we, a global elite, had adopted to shape the world seems to be crumbling. We believed that globalization and free trade would lift all boats. We believed that technology would make the world better for everyone. Innovation, along with globalization and technology, became a buzzword amongst us, and we limited the concept of innovation to the use of more technology. Thomas Friedman celebrated these trends in his bestselling book *The World is Flat: A Brief History of the Twenty-First Century*, published in 2005.[28] He was a celebrity at the World Economic Forum in Davos, shortly before the global financial crisis, when innovations in financial instruments, enabled by technology, shook up the world. The twenty-first century Friedman had predicted turned out to be very brief indeed.

Friedman launched his book in India because it was inspired, he said, by a revelation he had while playing golf in Bengaluru (then Bangalore) with one of the co-founders of Infosys, the globally admired Indian IT company. He said he saw hoardings of global brands around Bengaluru, such as Sony and Microsoft, and he could call his wife in the US from Bengaluru from his mobile phone. People in the city were connected with people everywhere in the world, he said. Ergo, the world is flat. Except that, as Mani Shankar Aiyar, who was then India's Minister of Panchayati Raj (Village Self-Government),

---

[28] Friedman, Thomas, *The World is Flat: A Brief History of the Twenty-First Century*, Farrar, Straus and Giroux, 2005.

pointed out sarcastically at the launch of Friedman's book in Delhi, 'People like us in Bangalore knew what was happening in New York, London and Tokyo, but did not know what was happening in villages just a few kilometres outside their cities.'

Philosopher Michael J. Sandel, a widely respected authority on democratic governance, analyses the state of democracy in the US in his book *Public Philosophy*—a collection of his essays on morality and politics.[29] He explains how the growth of liberal political philosophy has spurred ideas of individual rights and individualism. He observes how, in the market economy, human beings are becoming schooled to become smart consumers (and producers), but appear to be losing orientations and skills for citizenship in communities. Consequently, social solidarity is reducing. Political scientist Robert D. Putnam has also written about this trend eloquently in *Bowling Alone: The Collapse and Revival of the American Community* (Simon and Schuster, 2000).

Two centuries ago, French sociologist and political theorist, Alexis de Tocqueville, travelled to the US to study its institutions. He seemed most impressed with institutions of local self-governance in the American towns. In his book *Democracy in America*, published in 1835, he observed that participation in local affairs with their fellow citizens enables them to learn and practice the art of democratic government. In the same vein, Sandel (and even Putnam) explain the urgency, in an age of increasing anxiety, to strengthen intermediate

---

[29] Sandel, Michael J., *Public Philosophy: Essays on Morality in Politics*, Harvard University Press, 2005.

institutions between the individual and the nation—families and neighbourhood associations in villages and towns—for people to become more connected with others and more in control of the forces that shape their lives.

Technology-empowered algorithms are enabling owners of social media platforms, marketers and advertisers (even governments) to listen very sharply to each one of us. Interactions with each other, in intermediate institutions, can make us listen to each other.

With this analysis, some assertions may now be made about the structures and processes required for a healthy democracy. Firstly, a popular view of democracy—that it is principally a system of fair (and frequent) elections to determine the will of the majority—which is projected in TV images of people lining up at polling booths in Afghanistan, Iraq, and other such newly 'democratized' countries in George Bush's campaign to spread democracy through the world, is a dangerously facile view. Secondly, to remain healthy, democracies will require more devolution, and the participation of many more people in democratic institutions to counter the pressures from the erosion of national institutions on the one hand, and the rise of liberal, individualistic values on the other. Therefore, many more people will have to participate in deliberations, in many forums, to democratically determine policies that affect their lives. This leads to the conclusion that the quality of their deliberations and their respect for others' views, and not the fairness of elections, may be the key to effective democracy.

The design of a democratic structure—constitutions,

devolved institutions and electoral processes—is important for the democracy to function smoothly. However, the nature of the dialogue and deliberations of citizens within (and outside) these structures establishes that democracy's quality. The structures of institutions—elected bodies and independent judiciaries—and electoral processes are like the walls and doors and systems of the house. Or like the hardware of a computer. Dialogue and deliberations are the software of a democracy. And, as in computer systems, given adequate hardware, the system's performance depends entirely on the quality of the software. The software of a democracy is the process of democratic deliberation where people listen to the aspirations and views of people not like themselves.

HOW ON EARTH WILL WE LIVE TOGETHER?

11

SHAPING OUR FUTURE TOGETHER

I shall be telling this with a sigh
Somewhere ages and ages hence:
Two roads diverged in a wood, and I—
I took the one less traveled by,
And that has made all the difference.

—Robert Frost, 'The Road Not Taken'

I began the book with the story of an American Jesuit priest who listened very deeply to a foundry manager in India. He demonstrated the transformative power of listening for the well-being of the person who was listened to, as well as the power of listening to change the quality of relationships amongst a management team. In examples in the chapters that followed, the number of persons engaged in conversations with each other increased—from dozens in the union-employer deliberations about labour reforms and in the meetings of India's NDC, to hundreds during face-to-face meetings of citizens about the future of India, and to millions in conversations on social media.

Later in the book we visited Henry David Thoreau's cabin by Walden Pond, in which he had set three chairs—one for solitude, two for conversations and three for society. Then we stepped outside his cabin into the wide world of large, democratic societies and public discourse in the media and on the Internet. We have observed how the richness of conversations seems to diminish inevitably when it becomes larger. The further the conversations reach and the larger they become, the higher they rise out of the depths of dialogues that can build trust amongst people with different cultures and different identities, to the shallows of twittering and trolling on social media.

We have looked into the backs of our heads and seen structures within our minds that affect the ways in which we see the world and gauge others. They shape the 'lenses' through which we see the world. Diversity amongst the histories, cultures, races and even the type of education people receive, causes people to wear different lenses. Through their own lenses, they see different views of the same one reality. Each of us sees only a filtered and partial truth. We have to understand others' perspectives too, to be able to comprehend reality in its fullness.

We have also seen how the design of structures in which conversations happen—their settings and the design of processes—impact the quality of listening in conversations. Settings of conversations matter. Even the arrangements of the chairs can have an impact, and can change typical conversations amongst the societal and ideological 'positions' of participants, towards deeper conversations amongst who they are as 'persons'.

Even more than the design of the space and the layout, we have seen how the design of the *process* of the conversation influences the depth to which a conversation will go and how much listening there is. We saw distinctions between debates, deliberations and dialogues. Listening is deepest in dialogues.

Humanity is at crossroads. On one road, we will carry on with more of the same kind of conversation we are having, and merely make them larger with the technological prowess of social media. On this road, we will have even more conversations amongst people like ourselves, who see the world through the same lenses, and who are on 'our side'. On the same road we will also have more heated debates with others to prove them wrong, until we give them up as of no use to us, and return to the comfort of more conversations amongst people like us. Or, we can take the other road—the one 'grassy and wanting wear', the 'road less travelled by', in the words of Robert Frost in his poem 'The Road Not Taken'. On the road less travelled by, we will encounter the unfamiliar. We will be amongst people not like ourselves. We will see other views of our reality through their lenses. On this road, we will have to shake off the comforts of the stereotypes we have in our minds that make it so easy for us to pass quick judgements.

We saw in the previous chapter that richness cannot be brought into large-scale conversations which have the reach that democracies require unless meetings with face-to-face listening are included in the overall architecture of public conversation. James Madison and others, who developed the federal architecture of the US institutions, recognized the need for forums in which people could listen to different perspectives and deliberate thoughtfully. The quality of the meetings in these forums would provide the glue to keep a diverse and dynamic society together. Many of these forums would be local—in meetings of the towns' citizens. And other meetings would be in chambers of the representatives chosen by citizens in the State and Federal governments.

Constitutions can be redesigned, and new institutions can be created at national and international levels, with the intention of more collaboration amongst people. Unless there is more real listening to others' views in these forums with the willingness to change one's own, the world will not be improved. The ability to listen deeply to others not like ourselves is the answer to the question, 'How on Earth can we live together harmoniously and also harmoniously with the one Earth we share?'

The cultivation of skills for deeper listening begins with listening to the stranger who is within us. We hardly ever listen to our own minds.

EPILOGUE
AM I LISTENING?

It is the province of knowledge to speak and it is the privilege of wisdom to listen.

—Oliver Wendell Holmes

When my book *Shaping the Future: Aspirational Leadership in India and Beyond* (John Wiley and Sons, 2002) was published, the Confederation of Indian Industry (CII) invited me to speak to CEOs of India's largest companies in a series of breakfast meetings. I was cautioned that since the CEOs are busy people, the meetings would be for only an hour each. They did not want long monologues, but wanted to discuss ideas. I must get to the point very quickly or they would lose interest.

I began the meetings with a very brief, 10-minute description of the state of the world. Then I asked the CEOs a question: 'What do you care about most deeply?' Before anyone spoke or any hands came up, I suggested that they think of this question for a minute in silence. I said that in the answer to this question lay the possibility of them becoming transformative leaders.

I said that in my research of over 40 years into the essence of leadership, I had formulated a simple definition of a great leader. This was: 'A leader is he or she who takes the first steps towards what he or she cares about deeply and in ways that others then wish to follow.'

Great leaders in history had different profiles. Some were wealthy; some were very poor. Some had gone through an extensive formal education, while others did not finish school. Great leaders had different capabilities. Some were great orators; some were very shy. Therefore, I have found that lists, such as 'the ten skills of great leaders' or 'the seven things you must do to become a good leader', which many consultants offer (often with accompanying manuals and courses about how these skills and habits can be developed), do not get to the essence of what is required to lead change.

We loosely call people with positions of authority on top of formal institutions, in government and business sectors, as 'leaders'. We also loosely call wealthy people as leaders of society. The power of transformative leadership, I believe, does not arise from one's position or one's wealth. It comes from something within the leader. In the meeting, I presented a picture of Mahatma Gandhi leading Indians on the march to freedom. He did not have a stick of authority to order people to follow him, or any wealth to provide people with incentives to follow him. He could not use any conventional 'carrot and stick'. Yet people followed him. Because he cared for something they cared for too. They knew what he cared for. They could know this because he himself knew deeply what he cared for and devoted his life to that cause. Indeed, the title of his autobiography is *My Experiments with Truth*.

I suggested to the assembled CEOs that their discovery and reaffirmation of what they cared about most of all is the key to them becoming successful and great leaders. With that, I suggested to them that it may be worthwhile to reflect quietly on what they cared for the most. They should put off their phones, set aside their pens and papers, and perhaps shut their eyes for a couple of minutes to avoid distractions. All the CEOs agreed that a few minutes of this exercise was worthwhile. There was no harm in trying it, and they shut their eyes.

After three or four minutes, I asked them to open their eyes and give me their attention again. They had come out of their inner reflection, and some looked at each other silently. I asked them if they would like to know what their neighbour in the room cared about. And if they might also be willing to share with him or her what they themselves cared about. They all agreed. I urged them to look their partner in the eye as she or he said what they cared the most about and why, without interrupting them. And then to allow their partner to hear what they cared about. They did this in pairs, and then some spontaneously turned to their neighbours on the other side to listen to them too.

After ten or fifteen minutes, I asked them to give me their attention again and enquired what the few minutes of listening to each other had felt like. It was surprising, many revealed, that they had discovered something about themselves they hardly ever had time to reflect about. They also insisted that the experience of having their heartfelt thoughts being listened to by another person was very refreshing. This was similar to what the Telco foundry manager had also said after Father Joe Curry had listened to him.

The CEOs in these meetings were amongst similar people ('people like us') with similar education, responsibilities and broadly similar lifestyles. On the other hand, the over one hundred persons who met in the Jaipur Conclave (in Chapter 5) were very diverse: CEOs, politicians, bureaucrats, farmers, teachers, leaders of NGOs, students, journalists, homemakers and diplomats; women in silk saris and farmers in cotton dhotis; boys in school blazers and the Chief Minister of the state too. After explaining the purpose of the meeting at its opening, I asked them all the same question I had asked the CEOs: 'What do you care about most of all?' I asked them to reflect on this quietly, as I had asked the CEOs, and then to listen to their neighbours sitting beside them. They listened to each other in pairs. The Chief Minister listened to a young schoolboy, and he to her. A farmer and a CEO listened to each other. Then they gathered into larger groups of four and five. I let them go on. They were meeting each other in ways they had never met before.

When I asked the people in the Conclave what had absorbed them so much, they said, as the CEOs had too, that it was very refreshing to listen to another and to be listened to. Moreover, they were heartened to learn that, though they were so diverse, deep down they cared for the same things. There were bonds that united them in spite of their differences. The discovery

EPILOGUE AM I LISTENING?

of their common caring enabled them to listen to each other's points of view over the next two days, and to debate their many disagreements with less rancour.

LEVELS OF LISTENING

Listening to others is not easy when what they say seems so wrong. It may seem wrong because others see the same reality through different lenses. Like the blind men around the elephant, each of us is convinced that what we see is the truth, which it may be. But it is not the whole truth.

The first level of listening is to pay attention to 'what' the other person is saying, even if one does not agree. The instinct of a debater is to get ready with a riposte to prove the other wrong. Therefore, a debater stops listening even while the other is speaking.

Unlike a good debater, a good listener listens well to what the other is saying and also 'listens' to her own mind's reactions to it. She notices her disagreement, and her desire to counter the other. But she stops herself, and goes into a second and deeper level of listening. At this level, she wonders 'why' the other thinks the way he does. And, rather than debate the other, she asks the other, with genuine interest, 'Why do you believe what you do?' Thus, she begins to inquire into another's way of thinking, and begins to see the 'lens' through which the other sees the world.

From this second level, deep listeners come to a third, even more profound level of listening. Here, the listener begins to notice the difference between her own way of seeing the world and the other's. Thus, she may begin to see her own lens. Our lenses are our ways of seeing and thinking. They are buried in the backs of our minds. We cannot see them with our own eyes. However, we may see them reflected in the eyes of another. Deep listening makes one aware of 'who' another is. It also brings self-awareness about who we are.

Listening is for the health of a society like breathing is for the health of the body. Breathing tones up the mind and the organs of the body. Listening unclogs conversations and tones up democratic institutions. A good yoga teacher trains his pupil to breathe well. Then, he encourages her to concentrate on her breathing for a few moments each day: sitting on a chair at home, or even while travelling in the subway. Similarly, listening can be practiced everywhere: in a conversation with one's spouse, a discussion amongst a few friends, deliberations amongst stakeholders in a project, in small meetings, and in large conventions too.

The more we listen to each other, and the better we get at it, the faster and further we will go on 'the road less travelled by' so far. This we must, if we want to improve the world for everyone, and make a better world for ourselves too.

The question, 'What sort of a world are we leaving behind for our grandchildren?' has become a cliché. We cannot continue to live as we are, and leave it to our children to produce a more inclusive, just, harmonious and sustainable world for our grandchildren.

We must change now. And we have no option: we must

EPILOGUE AM I LISTENING?

collaborate with others to shape our collective future. Let us listen to our own aspirations. We must also listen to the aspirations of people not like us for the better world that they want to leave for their grandchildren.

A PRAYER

YOU CAN SEE ME FROM YOUR HIGH PEAKS
HEAR ME IN YOUR VAST SILENCE
FEEL ME WITH YOUR CARESSING BREEZES.
I QUIETLY LISTEN
TO YOUR VOICE IN THE STREAM
WAITING FOR YOU TO FIND ME.

ARUN MAIRA, 1988

Acknowledgements

I must acknowledge all those who have helped me create this book. I must also acknowledge those who made me curious about the subjects I have explored in the book as well as those who gave me knowledge about these subjects.

The impetus for writing this book was provided by my friends in Rupa Publications in 2015 when I was finishing my previous book which Rupa published—*An Upstart in Government: Journeys of Change and Learning*. In that book, I had written about the need for government to listen more to citizens, and for citizens to listen to each other. In it I had included some pages from a short book that my grandson, Viren, who was seven years old then, had written, complete with his hand-drawn pictures, about what he thought the purpose of the Planning Commission, where I served as a Member, must be. To a question that he had posed in his book, 'Why is there a Planning Commission (or Community, as he called it)?' his response was: 'The Planning Community is where there will be someone for the poor people to talk to and then there will be a big change in their life.' Ritu Vajpeyi-Mohan, who was then with Rupa, and I agreed that a book dedicated to the idea of 'listening' as a discipline to make the

LISTENING FOR WELL-BEING

world a better place for everyone would be very interesting.

Kapish Mehra of Rupa persuaded me to write the book. Yamini Chowdhury helped with some very valuable suggestions about the structure of the book and by editing it. I thank Kapish and Yamini, and Tanima Saha and others in Rupa who have made this book possible. My special thanks to Ritabrata Joardar who provided the illustrations in this book.

'If you have a garden and a library, you have everything you need,' Marcus Tullius Cicero, one of Rome's greatest orators (c.106–c.43 BC) had said. When I was a schoolboy, my mother made me listen to my thoughts and to nature. She taught me how to listen by listening to a living garden and by reading her books. These were my only companions most of the time during my summer holidays, when we lived in a village in Uttar Pradesh. My mother never allowed me to express boredom. If I dared to, she would say, 'Go read my books.' So even as a schoolboy, I read books by Aldous Huxley, Bertrand Russel, Mahatma Gandhi, Rabindranath Tagore, Leo Tolstoy, Thoreau, and by many other great minds. And if I felt bored or overwhelmed by the books, I was sent to the garden to listen to the grass growing.

Sumant Moolgaokar, the Chairman of Tata Engineering and Locomotive Co. Ltd, my great mentor, nudged me to listen to others. He could walk with Kings without losing the common touch—Rudyard Kipling's words. He was curious about everyone he encountered during his frequent visits to the factory. He would stop to interact with a gardener and ask him what he was doing. He would converse with workers in

ACKNOWLEDGEMENTS

the machine shops and assembly lines to ask them who they were and what they were learning.

My mother and Sumant Moolgaokar encouraged me to listen. Later, many others taught me ways to listen even better. The first amongst them was Father Joe Curry, whom I have introduced and acknowledged in the very beginning of this book. Then others like the wonderful participants in the International Society of Organizational Learning who would assemble annually in Bretton Woods, in New Hampshire. Amongst them were my colleagues in Innovation Associates, whom I also mention in the book.

I have continued my interest in books, and have learned a lot about listening, democracy, dialogue and deliberation from many authors. I have quoted from several of these books and have acknowledged their authors too. There are many other great minds and books whose ideas have helped me understand the value of deep listening, as well as the processes for facilitating it. I humbly acknowledge that I have had a great many teachers, too many to list here.

Arun Maira
17 May 2017

Index

1991 reforms, 22

Aam aadmi, 3, 5
Aam Aadmi Party (AAP), 141
Acemoglu, Daron, 16
Ahluwalia, Montek Singh, 86, 89
Aiyar, Mani Shankar, 154
Alami, Musa, 76
Anachronism, 13
Anderson, Phil, 89
St Andrews, 91–93, 96
Arab Spring, xxvi, 127
Architecture of institutions, 144
Arrow, Kenneth, 89
Arthur, Brian, 89
Asian economies, rise of, 5
Aspen Seminar, 125–126
Athenian democracy, 147
Attention deficit disorder, 131
Augustin, xxi, 75

Banks, Murray, xviii

Barnes & Noble and Borders, 130
Benz, Daimler, xv
Bernie Sanders, 10, 152
Bharti Mazdur Sangh (BMS), 30
Big Brother, 14
Black money, surgical strike, 12
Brexit, 1, 4–5, 7–8, 10, 13, 45, 104, 135, 145, 148
 shocks of, 47
 two-tracked process, 111
Bridges
 building process, 112
 conversational, 108
 principal structures, 108
British Petroleum, 92
Brown, Dan, 72–73
Buddhist council, 117
Bureaucrats, 21, 62, 166
Burqa, 54, 69
Bush, George W., 57, 156

Calhoun, Craig, 7
Capitalism, 5, 7, 10, 124, 128
Carrol, Kathleen, 124
Caste system, 17, 74
Catholic Christians, 81
Centralization processes, 9
Chaturvedi, B.K., 86
China
  economic resurgence, 77
  fascinated the West, 77
  rise of, 14
Churchill, Winston, 9
Civil Society Organizations (CSOs), 36–43
Civilizational conflict, 81
Clash of cultures, 85
Clinton, Hillary, 10, 141
Club of Rome, xxviii
CNN, 116
Collins, Randall, 7
Commonwealth Games, 114
Communism, 5, 138
Conceptually gated communities, 113, 132, 152
Confederation of Indian Industry (CII), 29, 35, 163
Constitution of India, xxx, 11, 18, 75, 147, 149
  declarations of equality, 74
Cook, Michael, 16–17
Coping strategy, 132

Corporate capitalism, 10, 13
  Davos version, 13
Cultivation of skills, 162
Cultural lenses, 73–82
  belief in the superiority, 75
  declarations of equality, 74
  geography, 74
Curry, Joe, xviii, xxii, xxv, 31, 75, 166

Dag Hammarskjold Foundation, xxv
Dalai Lama, 97, 119–120
Dead-end discourse, 28
Deep democracy, xxxi
Deliberation, 60, 65, 109, 118–119, 146–147, 149–150
Deliberative democracy, 8, 146, 148, 151–157
Democracy
  Athenian, 147
  deep, xxxi
  deliberative, 8, 146, 148, 151–157
  deterioration of, 148
  direct, 148
  discord within, 146–152
    deliberation, 147
    democratic deliberation, 146
    mass participation, 147
    political equality, 146–147

majoritarian, 144
popular view of, 156
Democratic deliberation, xxxi, 8, 44, 108, 123, 146–147, 152, 157
Democratic institutions, purpose of, 144
Demographic dividend, 23, 113
Demonetization, 11
Derluguian, Georgi, 7
Dictatorship, 16
Digital technology, 46
Direct democracy, 148
Diversity, 15, 62, 81, 105, 143, 160
Dubey, Rajeev, 29
Dvorak, Petr, 126
Dynasties, 5

E-commerce, 130
Economic measures of growth, 6
Economic reforms, 22, 114
Edelman Trust Barometer, 115
Educated elite, 149
Eisler, Riane, 72
Electoral democracies, 10
Employers' Federation of India, 29
Enlightenment
driver of the, 87
principal driver of, 87

science-driven, 87
scientific, 4
Environmental resources, 6
Epistemic Lenses, 70, 82–83
European Union (EU), xxvii, 4, 7
Evans, Robert, 57

Face-to-face listening, 161
Financialization of economies, 10, 153
Fishkin, James, 146
Five Star movement in Italy, 153
Five Year Plan, 21, 37, 44, 86
Flight of the Flamingos, 43
Foa, Roberto, xxvii
Forum 2000, 126–127, 137
Fox News, 116
Free and fair elections, xxxi
Free markets, ideologies, xxvi
Freedom of speech, 47
French Revolution of 1789, 14–15
Friedman, Milton, 128
Friedman, Thomas, 154
Frost, Robert, 112, 159, 161
Fukuyama, Francis, xxvi, 16
Fundamentalism, 120

Gandhi, Indira, 4
Gandhi, Priyanka, 3

Gandhi, Sonia, 3
Gell-Mann, Murray, 89
Gender lenses, 70–73
Geopolitics, 14
Ghonim, Wael, 127
Global problems, 44–48
Governance, reforms in, 114
Gray, John, 71
Gupta, Kavita, 24–26
Gurion, Ben, 76

Hameed, Syeda, 37, 85
Handy, Charles, 133–134
Hanh, Thich Nhat, xv
Havel, Vaclav, 126, 143
Heierbacher, Sandy, 118
Higgins, Henry, 71
Hinduism, 17
Hire and fire, 24
Hiroshima and Nagasaki, devastation of, 76
Hirschman, Albert O., 128
Holmes, Oliver Wendell, 163
Homogenization, processes of, 9
Humanity, 47, 128, 161
Huntington, Samuel P., 81–82

Icarus scenario,
Ideological conflicts, 14
Indian Space Research Organization (ISRO), 85

Industry associations, 21, 24–25, 29
Inequality, 44, 74, 153
Institute for Democracy and Electoral Assistance, 143
Integrative enlightenment, 91–96
International Futures Forum, 93
International Society of Organizational Learning, xxiv
Internet revolution, 130
ISIS, 8

Jaipur Conclave, 166
James, Michael Rabinder, 151
Jayalalithaa, J., 60
Jefferson, Thomas, 123
Joan, Miller, 80
Jobless growth, 23
Jones, Bobby, 92

Kagan, Robert, xxvi
Kahane, Adam, 42
Kapur, Surinder, 29
Kasturirangan, Krishnaswamy, 85–86, 89
Keen, Andrew, 131
Kejriwal, Arvind, 141
Kent, Thomas, 126
Kipling, Rudyard, 83

INDEX

Kleeman, Sophie, 143

Labour contractors, hiring workers, 24
Labour exploitation, 27
Labour laws, administration of, 24
Labour reforms, 33, 159
Labour Unions, 21, 24, 42
Lame Duck scenario, 43
Lapham, Lewis H., 47
Lathem, Connery E., 112
Learning organizations, xxiv
Lehman Brothers, collapse of, 88
Levels of listening, 167–169
Levin, Jerry, 125
Liberal democracy, 105, 139
 ideologies, xxvi

Madison, James, 147, 161
Mahatma Gandhi, 9, 12, 33, 76, 164
Majoritarian democracy, 144
 problem with, 144–145
Mann, Michael, 7
Manufacturing sector, 23–24
Market planners, 68
Marketers and Pollsters, 68–69
Michael, James R., 152
Millennium Development Goals, xxix

Miller, Joan, 79
Misogyny, origins of, 72
Misperceptions, 28
Mitchell, Waldorp, M., 90
Mobocracy, 127
Modi, Narendra, 11–12, 15, 60
 surgical demonetization, 12
Mont Fleur scenarios, 42
Moral consciences of leaders, 140
Mounk, Yascha, xxvii
Muddling Along, 44
Mueller, John, 141
My Experiments with Truth, 165

National Coalition of Dialogue and Deliberation (NCDD), 118
National Development Council (NDC), 59–60, 102
 ignominy of meetings, 60
National identity, 17
Neighbourhood associations, 156
Neo-Liberal economists, 36
New Testament, 73
Nicklaus, Jack, 92
Nisbett, Richard E., 78
NITI Aayog, 59
Non-directive counselling, xxi
Non-directive listening, xxi

Non-violent movements, 12
Nuclear Suppliers Group (NSG), 7
Nylhom, Per, 126

Obama, Barack, 127
Occupy Wall Street Movement, 152
Oreskes, Michael, 124
Ostrich scenario,

Palmer, Arnold, 92
Panchayati Raj (Village Self-Government), 154
Peace of Westphalia, 4
Pehe, Jiri, 143
Pew Research, 103, 132
Planning Commission, 21, 30, 35–44, 59, 85–86, 88–89, 109, 114
  accountablity, 36
  charter, 85
  contributions, 40
  CSOs and, 39
  dominated by economists, 85
  experts, 35
  mandate of, 35
  organized public consultations, 36
  pro-Western and pro-business bias, 41
  up-to-date model of Indian economy, 88
  WNTA and, 37, 42
PLUs' (People Like Us), 113
Pollsters, 68, 103
  accuracy of predictions, 68
Popova, Maria, 138
Protestant Christians, 81
Public deliberation, 150
Public discourse, decline in the quality of, 46
Putnam, Hilary, 136
Putnam, Robert D., 155

Radical Islamic terrorism, 82
Rainbow nation, 43
Raje, Vasundhara, 63
Reclaiming Conversations, 102
Referendums, 145
Refugees, 18, 104
Rodrik, Dani, 7
Rogers, Carl, xviii, xxi
Rumsfeld, Donald, 14
Russian nationalism, resurgence of, 14
Rutgers University Report, 132
Ryan, Carolyn, 124–125

Sachs, Jeffrey, 150
Sacks, Jonathan, 107, 120
Sandberg, Sheryl, 132

INDEX

Sandel, Michael J., 6, 124, 155
Scenario Planning, 42–44
Scottish Council Foundation, 92–93
Second World War, 75–76, 82
   Japan's defeat, 75
Security Council, 7
Sen, Amartya, 117
Service sector, growth, 22
Singh, Manmohan, 21
Slum dwellers' association, 35
Smartphones, 46, 103, 115, 129, 131–132
Snow, C.P., 82–83
Social Media, xxvi, xxxi, 8, 45–47, 88, 97, 102–104, 116, 119, 124, 126–127, 130–135, 137, 139, 146, 156, 159–161
   disillusionment with, 127
   impact on quality of interpersonal relationships, xxvii
   principal thrust of, 134
   proliferation of, 136
   prolific users of, 132
Socialist economists, 36
Socratic Method, 117
Soviet Union, collaps of, xxvi, 13, 75, 153
Stereotyping, 68–69

Sustainable Development Goals, xxviii

Tagore, Rabindranath, 1, 49, 55, 113
Tannen, Barbara, 117
Tannen, Deborah, 47
Technology-empowered algorithms, 156
Thoreau, Henry David, 99, 160
Tocqueville, Alexis de, 155
Transformative leadership, 165
Transformative power of listening, 159
Trump, Donald, 5, 10–11, 47, 82, 103–104, 124, 134–136, 139, 141, 150–152
Trust deficit, 113–116
Turkle, Shirley, 46–47, 102

Underemployment, 23
Uniform national tax, 9
United States Declaration of Independence, 74
Upadhyay, Vrijesh, 30
US presidential elections, 45

Vaidyanathan, Lata, 64
Velvet Revolution, 126

Wada Na Todo Abhiyan

(WNTA), 36–39
Walden Pond, 99, 103, 130, 160
Waldorp, M. Mitchel, 89
Wallerstein, Immanuel, 5–7, 15, 153
Washington swamp, 10
Wilde, Oscar, 67
Win-Win Solutions, 28
World Economic Forum, 154

World Systems Analysis, 5, 15, 153
World Values Survey, xxvii, 115
WTO, 7

Yoga, xxi, 48, 77, 168
Zionism, 76
Zuckerberg, Mark, 129, 132, 134–135